Merry Christmas

BEST-LOVED
STORIES & CAROLS

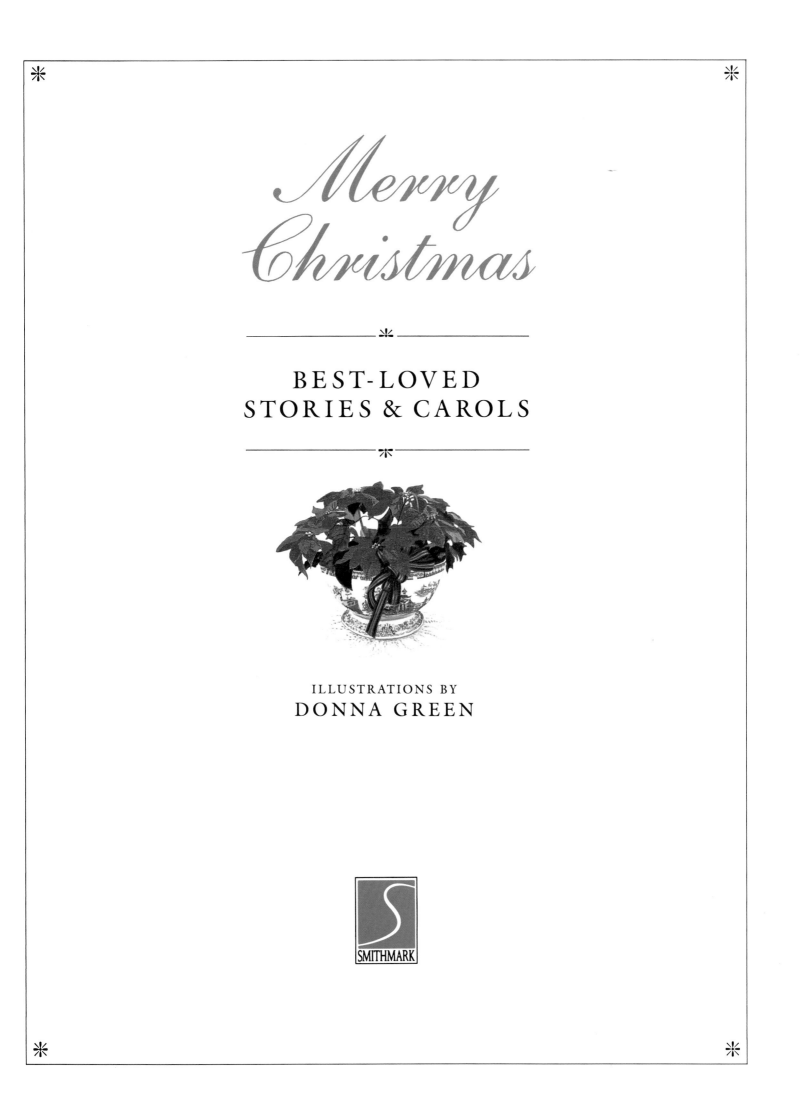

ILLUSTRATIONS BY
DONNA GREEN

SMITHMARK

*For Bob, whose
love and support
made this book possible.*

This edition first published in the United States of America in 1990 under the title
We Wish You a Merry Christmas by SMITHMARK Publishers, a division of
U.S. Media Holdings, Inc., 115 West 18th Street, New York, NY 10011.
Revised edition published in 1992 under the title *Merry Christmas.*

SMITHMARK books are available for bulk purchase for sales promotions and
premium use. For details write or telephone the manager of special sales,
SMITHMARK Publishers, a division of U.S. Media Holdings, Inc.,
115 West 18th Street, New York, NY 10011; (212) 532-6600.

A Rob Fremont Book

Editor: Deanne Urmy
Design by Carol Belanger Grafton
Composition: Trufont Typographers, Inc.
Music engraved by A-R Editions, Inc.

ISBN: 0-8317-6005-2

Printed and bound in Singapore by Imago Publishing Ltd.

10 9 8 7 6 5 4

Contents

Stories

Carols

Christmas Underground

KENNETH GRAHAME

"What a capital little house this is!" Mr. Rat called out cheerily. "So compact! So well planned! Everything here and everything in its place! We'll make a jolly night of it. The first thing we want is a good fire; I'll see to that—I always know where to find things. So this is the parlor? Splendid! Your own idea, those little sleeping-bunks in the wall? Capital! Now, I'll fetch the wood and the coals, and you get a duster, Mole—you'll find one in the drawer of the kitchen table—and try and smarten things up a bit. Bustle about, old chap!"

Encouraged by his inspiriting companion, the Mole roused himself and dusted and polished with energy and heartiness, while the Rat, running to and fro with armfuls of fuel, soon had a cheerful blaze roaring up the chimney. He hailed the Mole to come and warm himself; but Mole promptly had another fit of the blues, dropping down on a couch in dark despair and burying his face in his duster.

"Rat," he moaned, "how about your supper, you poor, cold, hungry, weary animal? I've nothing to give you—nothing—not a crumb!"

"What a fellow you are for giving in!" said the Rat reproachfully. "Why, only just now I saw a sardine-opener on the kitchen dresser, quite distinctly; and everybody knows that means there are sardines about somewhere in the neighborhood. Rouse yourself! pull yourself together, and come with me and forage."

They went and foraged accordingly, hunting through every cupboard and turning out every drawer. The result was not so very depressing after all, though of course it might have been better; a tin of sardines—a box of captain's biscuits, nearly full—and a German sausage encased in silver paper.

"There's a banquet for you!' observed the Rat, as he arranged the table. "I know some animals who would give their ears to be sitting down to supper with us tonight!"

"No bread!" groaned the Mole dolorously; "no butter, no—"

"No *pâté de foie gras*, no champagne!" continued the Rat, grinning. "And that reminds me—what's that little door at the end of the passage? Your cellar, of course! Every luxury in this house! Just you wait a minute."

He made for the cellar door, and presently re-appeared, somewhat dusty, with a bottle of beer in each paw and another under each arm. "Self-indulgent beggar you seem to be, Mole," he observed. "Deny yourself nothing. This is really the jolliest little place I ever was in. Now, wherever did you pick up those prints? Make the place look so home-like, they do. No wonder you're so fond of it, Mole. Tell us all about it, and how you came to make it what it is."

Then, while the Rat busied himself fetching plates, and knives and forks, and mustard which he mixed in an egg-cup, the Mole, his bosom still heaving with the stress of his recent emotion, related—somewhat shyly at first, but with more freedom as he warmed to his subject—how this was planned, and how that was

1

thought out, and how this was got through a windfall from an aunt, and that was a wonderful find and a bargain, and this other thing was bought out of laborious savings and a certain amount of "going without." His spirits finally quite restored, he must needs go and caress his possessions, and take a lamp and show off their points to his visitor, and expatiate on them, quite forgetful of the supper they both so much needed; Rat, who was desperately hungry but strove to conceal it, nodding seriously, examining with a puckered brow, and saying, "Wonderful," and "Most remarkable," at intervals, when the chance for an observation was given him.

At last the Rat succeeded in decoying him to the table, and had just got seriously to work with the sardine-opener when sounds were heard from the forecourt without—sounds like the scuffling of small feet in the gravel and a confused murmur of tiny voices, while broken sentences reached them—"Now, all in a line—hold the lantern up a bit, Tommy—clear your throats first—no coughing after I say one, two, three.—Where's young Bill?—Here, come on, do, we're all a-waiting—"

"What's up?" inquired the Rat, pausing in his labors.

"I think it must be the field-mice," replied the Mole, with a touch of pride in his manner. "They go round carol-singing regularly at this time of the year. They're quite an institution in these parts. And they never pass me over—they come to Mole End last of all; and I used to give them hot drinks, and supper sometimes, when I could afford it. It will be like old times to hear them again."

"Let's have a look at them!" cried the Rat, jumping up and running to the door.

It was a pretty sight, and a seasonable one, that met their eyes when they flung the door open. In the forecourt, lit by the dim rays of a horn lantern, some eight or ten little field-mice stood in a semi-circle, red worsted comforters round their throats, their forepaws thrust deep into their pockets, their feet jigging for warmth. With bright beady eyes they glanced shyly at each other, sniggering a little, sniffing and applying coatsleeves a good deal. As the door opened, one of the elder ones that carried the lantern was just saying, "Now then, one, two, three!" and forthwith their shrill little voices uprose on the air, singing one of the old-time carols that their forefathers composed in fields that were fallow and held by frost, or when snow-bound in chimney corners, and handed down to be sung in the miry street to lamp-lit windows at Yule-time.

Villagers all, this frosty tide,
Let your doors swing open wide,
Though wind may follow, and snow beside,
Yet draw us in by your fire to bide;
    Joy shall be yours in the morning!

Here we stand in the cold and the sleet,
Blowing fingers and stamping feet,
Come from far away you to greet—
You by the fire and we in the street—
    Bidding you joy in the morning!

For ere one half of the night was gone,
Sudden a star has led us on,
Raining bliss and benison—
Bliss tomorrow and more anon,
    Joy for every morning!

Goodman Joseph toiled through the snow—
Saw the star o'er a stable low;
Mary she might not further go—
Welcome thatch, and litter below!
    Joy was hers in the morning!

And when they heard the angels tell
"Who were the first to cry Nowell?
Animals all, as it befell,
In the stable where they did dwell!
    Joy shall be theirs in the morning!"

The voices ceased, the singers, bashful but smiling, exchanged sidelong glances, and silence succeeded—but for a moment only. Then, from up above and far away, down the tunnel they had so lately travelled was

borne to their ears in a faint musical hum the sound of distant bells ringing a joyful and clangorous peal.

"Very well sung, boys!" cried the Rat heartily. "And now come along in, all of you, and warm yourselves by the fire, and have something hot!"

"Yes, come along, field-mice," cried the Mole eagerly. "This is quite like old times! Shut the door after you. Pull up that settle to the fire. Now, you just wait a minute, while we—O, Ratty!" he cried in despair, plumping down on a seat, with tears impending. "Whatever are we doing? We've nothing to give them!"

"You leave all that to me," said the masterful Rat. "Here, you with the lantern! Come over this way. I want to talk to you.

"Now, tell me, are there any shops open at this hour of the night?"

"Why, certainly, sir," replied the field-mouse respectfully. "At this time of the year our shops keep open to all sorts of hours."

"Then look here!" said the Rat. "You go off at once, you and your lantern, and you get me—"

Here much muttered conversation ensued, and the Mole only heard bits of it, such as—"Fresh, mind!—no, a pound of that will do—see you get Buggins's, for I won't have any other—no, only the best—if you can't get it there, try somewhere else—yes, of course, home-made, no tinned stuff—well then, do the best you can!" Finally, there was a chink of coin passing from paw to paw, the field-mouse was provided with an ample basket for his purchases, and off he hurried, he and his lantern.

The rest of the field-mice, perched in a row on the settle, their small legs swinging, gave themselves up to the enjoyment of the fire, and toasted their chilblains till they tingled; while the Mole, failing to draw them into easy conversation, plunged into family history and made each of them recite the names of his numerous brothers, who were too young, it appeared, to be allowed to go out a-carolling this year, but looked forward very shortly to winning the parental consent.

The Rat, meanwhile, was busy examining the label on one of the beer-bottles. "I perceive this to be Old Burton," he remarked approvingly. "*Sensible* Mole! The very thing! Now we shall be able to mull some ale! Get the things ready, Mole, while I draw the corks."

It did not take long to prepare the brew and thrust the tin heater well into the red heart of the fire; and soon every field-mouse was sipping and coughing and choking (for a little mulled ale goes a long way) and wiping his eyes and laughing and forgetting he had ever been cold in all his life.

"They act plays too, these fellows," the Mole explained to the Rat. "Make them up all by themselves, and act them afterwards. And very well they do it, too! They gave us a capital one last year, about a field-mouse who was captured at sea by a Barbary corsair, and made to row in a galley; and when he escaped and got home again, his lady-love had gone into a convent. Here, *you*! You were in it, I remember. Get up and recite a bit."

The field-mouse addressed got up on his legs, giggled shyly, looked round the room, and remained absolutely tongue-tied. His comrades cheered him on, Mole coaxed and encouraged him, and the Rat went so far as to take him by the shoulders and shake him; but nothing could overcome his stage-fright. They were all busily engaged on him like watermen applying the Royal Humane Society's regulations to a case of long submersion, when the latch clicked, the door opened, and the field-mouse with the lantern re-appeared, staggering under the weight of his basket.

There was no more talk of play-acting once the very real and solid contents of the basket had been tumbled out on the table. Under the generalship of Rat, everybody was set to do something or to fetch something. In a very few minutes supper was ready, and Mole, as he took the head of the table in a sort of dream, saw a lately barren board set thick with savory comforts; saw his little friends' faces brighten and beam as they fell to without delay; and then let himself loose—for he was famished indeed—on the provender so magically provided, thinking what a happy home-coming this had turned out, after all. As they ate, they talked of old times, and the field-mice gave him the local gossip up to date, and answered as well as they could the hundred questions he had to ask them. The Rat said little or nothing, only taking care that each guest had what he wanted, and plenty of it, and that Mole had no trouble or anxiety about anything.

They clattered off at last, very grateful and showering wishes of the season, with their jacket pockets stuffed with remembrances for the small brothers and sisters at home. When the door had closed on the last of them and the chink of the lanterns had died away, Mole and Rat kicked the fire up, drew their chairs in, brewed themselves a last nightcap of mulled ale, and discussed the events of the long day. At last the Rat, with a tremendous yawn, said, "Mole, old chap, I'm ready to drop. Sleepy is simply not the word. That your own bunk over on that side? Very well, then, I'll take this. What a ripping little house this is! Everything so handy!"

He clambered into his bunk and rolled himself well up in the blankets, and slumber gathered him forthwith, as a swath of barley is folded into the arms of the reaping-machine.

The weary Mole also was glad to turn in without delay, and soon had his head on his pillow, in great joy and contentment. But ere he closed his eyes he let them wander round his old room, mellow in the glow of the firelight that played or rested on familiar and friendly things which had long been unconsciously a part of him, and now smilingly received him back, without rancor. He was now in just the frame of mind that the tactful Rat had quietly worked to bring about in him. He saw clearly how plain and simple—how narrow, even—it all was; but clearly, too, how much it all meant to him, and the special value of some such anchorage in one's existence. He did not at all want to abandon the new life and its splendid spaces, to turn his back on sun and air and all they offered him and creep home and stay there; the upper world was all too strong, it called to him still, even down there, and he knew he must return to the larger stage. But it was good to think he had this to come back to, this place which was all his own, these things which were so glad to see him again and could always be counted upon for the same simple welcome.

from *The Wind in the Willows*

Carols in Gloucestershire

LAURIE LEE

*L*ater, towards Christmas, there was heavy snow, which raised the roads to the top of the hedges. There were millions of tons of the lovely stuff, plastic, pure, all-purpose, which nobody owned, which one could carve or tunnel, eat, or just throw about. It covered the hills and cut off the villages, but nobody thought of rescues; for there was hay in the barns and flour in the kitchens, the woman baked bread, the cattle were fed and sheltered—we'd been cut off before, after all.

The week before Christmas, when snow seemed to lie thickest, was the moment for carol-singing; and when I think back to those nights it is to the crunch of snow and to the lights of the lanterns on it. Carol-singing in my village was a special tithe for the boys, the girls had little to do with it. Like hay-making, black-berrying, stone-clearing and wishing-people-a-happy-Easter, it was one of our seasonal perks.

By instinct we knew just when to begin it; a day too soon and we should have been unwelcome, a day too late and we should have received lean looks from people whose bounty was already exhausted. When the true moment came, exactly balanced, we recognized it and were ready.

So as soon as the wood had been stacked in the oven to dry for the morning fire, we put on our scarves and went out through the streets, calling loudly between our hands, till the various boys who knew the signal ran out from their houses to join us.

One by one they came stumbling over the snow, swinging their lanterns around their heads, shouting and coughing horribly.

"Coming carol-barking then?"

We were the Church Choir, so no answer was necessary. For a year we had praised the Lord out of key, and as a reward for this service—on top of the Outing—we now had the right to visit all the big houses, to sing our carols and collect our tribute.

To work them all in meant a five-mile journey over wild and generally snowed-up country. So the first thing we did was to plan our route; a formality, as the route never changed. All the same, we blew on our fingers and argued; and then we chose our Leader. This was not binding, for we all fancied ourselves as Leaders, and he who started the night in that position usually trailed home with a bloody nose.

Eight of us set out that night. There was Sixpence the Simple, who had never sung in his life (he just worked his mouth in Church); the brothers Horace and Boney, who were always fighting everybody and always getting the worst of it; Clergy Green, the preaching maniac; Walt the bully, and my two brothers. As we went down the lane other boys, from other villages, were already about the hills, bawling "Kingwenslush", and shouting through keyholes "Knock on the knocker! Ring at the Bell! Give us a penny for singing so well!" They weren't an approved charity as we were, the Choir; but competition was in the air.

Our first call as usual was the house of the Squire, and we trouped nervously down his drive. For light we had candles in marmalade-jars suspended on loops of string, and they threw pale gleams on the towering snowdrifts that stood on each side of the drive. A blizzard was blowing, but we were well wrapped up, with Army puttees on our legs, woollen hats on our heads, and several scarves around our ears.

As we approached the Big House across its white silent lawns, we too grew respectfully silent. The lake near by was stiff and black, the waterfall frozen and still. We arranged ourselves shuffling around the big front door, then knocked and announced the Choir.

A maid bore the tidings of our arrival away into the echoing distances of the house, and while we waited we cleared our throats noisily. Then she came back, and the door was left ajar for us, and we were bidden to begin. We brought no music, the carols were in our heads. "Let's give 'em 'Wild Shepherds'," said Jack. We began in confusion, plunging into a wreckage of keys, of different words and tempo; but we gathered our strength; he who sang loudest took the rest of us with him, and the carol took shape if not sweetness.

This huge stone house, with its ivied walls, was always a mystery to us. What were those gables, those rooms and attics, those narrow windows veiled by the cedar trees? As we sang "Wild Shepherds" we craned our necks, gaping into that lamp-lit hall which we had never entered; staring at the muskets and untenanted chairs, the great tapestries furred by dust—until suddenly, on the stairs, we saw the old Squire himself standing and listening with his head on one side.

He didn't move until we'd finished; then slowly he tottered towards us, dropped two coins in our box with a trembling hand, scratched his name in the book we carried, gave us each a long look with his moist blind eyes, then turned away in silence.

As though released from a spell, we took a few sedate steps, then broke into a run for the gate. We didn't stop till we were out of the grounds. Impatient, at last, to discover the extent of his bounty, we squatted by the cowsheds, held our lanterns over the book, and saw that he had written "Two Shillings". This was quite a good start. No one of any worth in the district would dare to give us less than the Squire.

So with money in the box, we pushed on up the valley, pouring scorn on each other's performance. Confident now, we began to consider our quality and whether one carol was not better suited to us than another. Horace, Walt said, shouldn't sing at all; his voice was beginning to break. Horace disputed this and there was a brief token battle—they fought as they walked, kicking up divots of snow, then they forgot it, and Horace still sang.

Steadily we worked through the length of the valley, going from house to house, visiting the lesser and the greater gentry—the farmers, the doctors, the merchants, the majors and other exalted persons. It was freezing hard and blowing too; yet not for a moment did we feel the cold. The snow blew into our

faces, into our eyes and mouths, soaked through our puttees, got into our boots, and dripped from our woollen caps. But we did not care. The collecting-box grew heavier, and the list of names in the book longer and more extravagant, each trying to outdo the other.

Mile after mile we went, fighting against the wind, falling into snowdrifts, and navigating by the lights of the houses. And yet we never saw our audience. We called at house after house; we sang in courtyards and porches, outside windows, or in the damp gloom of hallways; we heard voices from hidden rooms; we smelt rich clothes and strange hot food; we saw maids bearing in dishes or carrying away coffee-cups; we received nuts, cakes, figs, preserved ginger, dates, cough-drops and money; but we never once saw our patrons. We sang as it were at the castle walls, and apart from the Squire, who had shown himself to prove that he was still alive, we never expected it otherwise.

As the night drew on there was trouble with Boney. "Noël", for instance, had a rousing harmony which Boney persisted in singing, and singing flat. The others forbade him to sing it at all, and Boney said he would fight us. Picking himself up, he agreed we were right, then he disappeared altogether. He just turned away and walked into the snow and wouldn't answer when we called him back. Much later, as we reached a far point up the valley, somebody said "Hark!" and we stopped to listen. Far away across the fields from the distant village came the sound of a frail voice singing, singing "Noël", and singing it flat—it was Boney, branching out on his own.

We approached our last house high up on the hill, the place of Joseph the farmer. For him we had chosen a special carol, which was about the other Joseph, so that we always felt that singing it added a spicy cheek to the night. The last stretch of country to reach his farm was perhaps the most difficult of all. In these rough bare lanes, open to all winds, sheep were buried and wagons lost. Huddled together, we tramped in one another's footsteps, powdered snow blew into our screwed-up eyes, the candles burnt low, some blew out altogether, and we talked loudly above the gale.

Crossing, at last, the frozen mill-stream—whose wheel in summer still turned a barren mechanism—we climbed up to Joseph's farm. Sheltered by trees, warm on its bed of snow, it seemed always to be like this. As always it was late; as always this was our final call. The snow had a fine crust upon it, and the old trees sparkled like tinsel.

We grouped ourselves round the farmhouse porch. The sky cleared, and broad streams of stars ran down over the valley and away to Wales. On Slad's white slopes, seen through the black sticks of its woods, some red lamps still burned in the windows.

Everything was quiet; everywhere there was the faint crackling silence of the winter night. We started singing, and we were all moved by the words and the sudden trueness of our voices. Pure, very clear, and breathless we sang:

As Joseph was a-walking	He neither shall be bornèd
He heard an angel sing;	In Housen nor in hall,
"This night shall be the birth-time	Nor in a place of paradise
Of Christ the Heavenly King.	But in an ox's stall. . . ."

And 2,000 Christmasses became real to us then; the houses, the halls, the places of paradise had all been visited; the stars were bright to guide the Kings through the snow; and across the farmyard we could hear the beasts in their stalls. We were given roast apples and hot mince-pies, in our nostrils were spices like myrrh, and in our wooden box, as we headed back for the village, there were golden gifts for all.

from *Cider With Rosie*

The Fir Tree

HANS CHRISTIAN ANDERSEN

Out in the forest stood a pretty little Fir Tree. It had a good place; it could have sunlight, air there was in plenty, and all around grew many larger comrades—pines as well as firs. But the little Fir Tree wished ardently to become greater. It did not care for the warm sun and the fresh air; it took no notice of the peasant children, who went about talking together when they had come out to look for strawberries and raspberries. Often they came with a whole potful, or had strung berries on a straw. Then they would sit down by the little Fir Tree and say, "How pretty and small that one is!" and the Tree did not like to hear that at all.

"Oh, if I were only as great a tree as the others!" sighed the little Fir. "Then I would spread my branches far around, and look out from my crown into the wide world. The birds would then build nests in my boughs, and when the wind blew, I could nod just as grandly as the others yonder."

He took no pleasure in the sunshine, in the birds, and in the red clouds that went sailing over him morning and evening. When it was winter and the snow lay all around, white and sparkling, a hare would often come jumping along, and spring right over the little Fir. Oh! this made him so angry. But two winters went by, and when the third came, the little Tree had grown so tall that the hare was obliged to run around it.

"Oh! to grow, to grow, and become old; that's the only fine thing in the world," thought the Tree.

In the autumn, woodcutters always came and felled a few of the largest trees; that was done this year too. And the little Fir Tree, which was now quite well grown, shuddered with fear, for the great stately trees fell to the ground with a crash, and their branches were cut off, so that the trees looked quite naked, long, and slender—they could hardly be recognized. But then they were laid upon wagons, and horses dragged them away out of the wood. Where were they going? What destiny awaited them?

In the spring, when the Swallows and the Stork came, the Tree asked them, "Do you know where they were taken? Did you not meet them?"

The Swallows knew nothing about it, but the Stork looked thoughtful, nodded his head, and said, "Yes, I think so. I met many new ships when I flew out of Egypt; on the ships were stately masts. I fancy that these were the trees. They smelt like fir. I can assure you they're stately—very stately."

"Oh, that I were only big enough to go over the sea! What kind of thing is this sea, and how does it look?"

"It would take too long to explain all that," said the Stork, and he went away.

"Rejoice in thy youth," said the Sunbeams. "Rejoice in thy fresh growth, and in the young life that is within thee."

And the wind kissed the Tree, and the dew wept tears upon it; but the Fir Tree did not understand that.

When Christmas time approached, quite young trees were felled, sometimes trees which were neither so old nor so large as this Fir Tree that never rested but always wanted to go away. These young trees, which were almost the most beautiful, kept all their branches; they were put upon wagons, and horses dragged them away out of the wood.

"Where are they all going?" asked the Fir Tree. "They are not greater than I—indeed one of them was much smaller. Why do they keep all their branches? Whither are they taken?"

"We know that! We know that!" chirped the Sparrows. "Yonder in the town we looked in at the windows. We know where they go. Oh! they are dressed up in the greatest pomp and splendor that can be imagined. We have looked in at the windows, and have perceived that they are planted in the middle of the warm room, and adorned with the most beautiful things—gilt apples, honey cakes, playthings, and many hundreds of candles."

"And then?" asked the Fir Tree, and trembled through all its branches. "And then? What happens then?"

"Why, we have not seen anything more," said the Sparrows. "But it was incomparable."

"Perhaps I may be destined to tread this glorious path one day!" cried the Fir Tree rejoicingly. "That is even better than travelling across the sea. How painfully I long for it! If it were only Christmas now! Now I am great and grown-up, like the rest who were led away last year. Oh, if I were only on the carriage! If I were only in the warm room, among all the pomp and splendor! And then? Yes, then something even better will come, something far more charming, or else why should they adorn me so? There must be something grander, something greater still to come, but what? Oh! I'm suffering, I'm longing! I don't know, myself, what is the matter with me!"

"Rejoice in us," said Air and Sunshine. "Rejoice in thy fresh youth here in the woodland."

But the Fir Tree did not rejoice at all, but it grew and grew. Winter and summer it stood there, green, dark green. The people who saw it said, "That's a handsome tree!" and at Christmas time it was felled before any one of the others. The axe cut deep into its marrow, and the tree fell to the ground with a sigh. It felt a pain, a sensation of faintness, and could not think at all of happiness, for it was sad at parting from its home, from the place where it had grown up. It knew that it should never again see the dear old companions, the little bushes and flowers all around—perhaps not even the birds. The parting was not at all agreeable.

The Tree only came to itself when it was unloaded in a yard, with the other trees, and heard a man say, "This one is perfect; we only want this one!"

Now two servants came, in gay liveries, and carried the Fir Tree into a large, beautiful saloon. All around the walls hung pictures, and by the great stove stood large Chinese vases with lions on the covers. There were rocking chairs, silken sofas, great tables covered with picture books, and toys worth a hundred times a hundred dollars—at least the children said so. And the Fir Tree was put into a great tub filled with sand; but no one could see that it was a tub, for it was hung round with green cloth, and stood on a large, many-colored carpet. Oh, how the Tree trembled! What was to happen now? The servants and the young ladies, also, decked it out. On one branch they hung little nets cut out of colored paper—every net was filled with sweetmeats; golden apples and walnuts hung down as if they grew there; and more than a hundred little candles, red, white, and blue, were fastened to the different boughs. Dolls that looked exactly like real people—the Tree had never seen such before—swung upon the foliage, and high on the summit of the Tree was fixed a tinsel star. It was splendid, particularly splendid.

"This evening," said all, "this evening it will shine."

"Oh," thought the Tree, "that it were evening already! Oh, that the lights may be soon lit up! When may that be done? I wonder if trees will come out of the forest to look at me? Will the Sparrows fly against the panes? Shall I grow fast here, and stand adorned in summer and winter?"

Yes, he did not guess badly. But he had a complete backache from mere longing, and the backache is just as bad for a tree as the headache for a person.

At last the candles were lighted. What a brilliance, what splendor! The Tree trembled so in all its branches that one of the candles set fire to a green twig, and it was scorched.

"Heaven preserve us!" cried the young ladies, and they hastily put the fire out.

Now the Tree might not even tremble. Oh, that was terrible! It was so afraid of setting fire to some of its ornaments, and it was quite bewildered with all the brilliance. And now the folding doors were thrown open, and a number of children rushed in as if they would have overturned the whole Tree; the older people followed more deliberately. The little ones stood quite silent, but only for a minute; then they shouted till the room rang.

They danced gleefully round the Tree, and one present after another was plucked from it.

"What are they about?" thought the Tree. "What's going to be done?"

And the candles burned down to the twigs, and as they burned down they were extinguished, and then the children received permission to plunder the Tree. Oh! they rushed in upon it, so that every branch cracked again. If the Tree had not been fastened by the top and by the golden star to the ceiling, it would have fallen down.

The children danced about with their pretty toys. No one looked at the Tree except one old man, who came up and peeped among the branches, but only to see if a fig or an apple had not been forgotten.

"A story! A story!" shouted the children, and they drew a little fat man toward the Tree, and he sat down just beneath it—"for then we shall be in the green wood," said he, "and the tree may have the advantage of listening to my tale. But I can only tell one. Will you hear the story of Ivede-Avede, or of Klumpey-Dumpey, who fell downstairs, and still was raised up to honor and married the Princess?"

"Ivede-Avede!" cried some. "Klumpey-Dumpey!" cried others. And there was a great crying and shouting. Only the Fir Tree was quite silent, and thought, "Shall I not be in it? Shall I have nothing to do in it?" But he had been in the evening's amusement, and had done what was required of him.

And the fat man told about Klumpey-Dumpey, who fell downstairs, and yet was raised to honor and married the Princess. And the children clapped their hands, and cried, "Tell another! Tell another!" for they wanted to hear about Ivede-Avede. But they only got the story of Klumpey-Dumpey. The Fir Tree stood quite silent and thoughtful; never had the birds in the wood told such a story as that. Klumpey-Dumpey fell downstairs, and yet came to honor and married the Princess!

"Yes, so it happens in the world!" thought the Fir Tree, and believed it must be true, because that was such a nice man who had told it. "Well, who can know? Perhaps I shall fall downstairs too, and marry a Princess!" And it looked forward with pleasure to being adorned again, the next evening, with candles and toys, gold and fruit. "Tomorrow I shall not tremble," it thought. "I will rejoice in all my splendor. Tomorrow I shall hear the story of Klumpey-Dumpey again and, perhaps, that of Ivede-Avede too." And the Tree stood all night, quiet and thoughtful.

In the morning the servants and the chambermaid came in.

"Now my splendor will begin afresh," thought the Tree. But they dragged him out of the room, and upstairs to the garret, and here they put him in a dark corner where no daylight shone.

"What's the meaning of this?" thought the Tree. "What am I to do here? What is to happen?"

And he leaned against the wall, and thought and thought. And he had time enough, for days and nights went by and nobody came up; and when at length someone came, it was only to put some great boxes in a corner. Now the Tree stood quite hidden away, and the supposition was that it was quite forgotten.

"Now it's winter outside," thought the Tree. "The earth is hard and covered with snow, and people cannot plant me. Therefore I suppose I'm to be sheltered here until spring comes. How considerate that is! How good people are! If it were only not so dark here, and so terribly solitary—not even a little hare! That was pretty out there in the wood, when the snow lay thick and the hare sprang past; yes, even when he jumped over me—but then I did not like it. It is terribly lonely up here!"

"Piep! Piep!" said a little Mouse, and crept forward. And then came another little one. They smelt at the Fir Tree, and then slipped among the branches.

"It's horribly cold," said the two little Mice, "or else it would be comfortable here. Don't you think so, you old Fir Tree?"

"I'm not old at all," said the Fir Tree. "There are many much older than I."

"Where do you come from?" asked the Mice. "And what do you know?" They were dreadfully inquisitive. "Tell us about the most beautiful spot on earth. Have you been there? Have you been in the storeroom, where the cheeses lie on the shelves and hams hang from the ceiling, where one dances on tallow candles, and goes in thin and comes out fat?"

"I don't know that!" replied the Tree. "But I know the wood, where the sun shines and where the birds sing."

And then it told all about its youth. The little Mice had never heard anything of the kind; and they listened and said, "What a number of things you have seen! How happy you must have been!"

"I?" said the Fir Tree, and it thought about what it had told. "Yes, those were really quite happy times." But then he told of the Christmas Eve, when he had been hung with sweetmeats and candles.

"Oh!" said the little Mice, "how happy you have been, you old Fir Tree!"

"I'm not old at all," said the Tree. "I only came out of the wood this winter. I'm only rather backward in my growth."

"What splendid stories you can tell!" said the little Mice.

And the next night they came with four other little Mice, to hear what the Tree had to relate. And the more it said, the more clearly did it remember everything, and thought, "Those were quite merry days! But they may come again. Klumpey-Dumpey fell downstairs, and yet he married the Princess. Perhaps I may marry a Princess too!" And then the Fir Tree thought of a pretty little Birch Tree that grew out in the forest. For the Fir Tree, that Birch was a real Princess.

"Who's Klumpey-Dumpey?" asked the little Mice.

And then the Fir Tree told the whole story. It could remember every single word, and the little Mice were ready to leap to the very top of the tree with pleasure. Next night a great many more Mice came, and on Sunday even two Rats appeared. But these thought the story was not pretty, and the little Mice were sorry for that, for now they also did not like it so much as before.

"Do you only know one story?" asked the Rats.

"Only that one," replied the Tree. "I heard it on the happiest evening of my life; I did not think then how happy I was."

"It's a very miserable story. Don't you know any about bacon and tallow candles—a storeroom story?"

"No," said the Tree.

"Then we'd rather not hear you," said the Rats. And they went back to their own people. The little Mice at last stayed away also, and then the Tree sighed and said, "It was very nice when they sat around me, the merry little Mice, and listened when I spoke to them. Now that's past too. But I shall remember to be pleased when they take me out."

But when did that happen? Why, it was one morning that people came and rummaged in the garret. The boxes were put away, and the Tree brought out. They certainly threw him rather roughly on the floor, but a servant dragged him away at once to the stairs, where the daylight shone.

"Now life is beginning again!" thought the Tree.

It felt the fresh air and the first sunbeams, and now it was out in the courtyard. Everything passed so quickly that the Tree quite forgot to look at itself, there was so much to look at all round. The courtyard

was close to a garden, and here everything was blooming. The roses hung fresh and fragrant over the little paling, the linden trees were in blossom, and the Swallows cried, "Quinze-wit! Quinze-wit! My husband's come!" But it was not the Fir Tree that they meant.

"Now I shall live!" said the Tree rejoicingly, and spread its branches far out. But, alas! they were all withered and yellow, and the Tree lay in the corner among nettles and weeds. The tinsel star was still upon it, and shone in the bright sunshine.

In the courtyard were playing a couple of the merry children who had danced round the Tree at Christmas time, and had rejoiced over it. One of the youngest ran up and tore off the golden star.

"Look what is sticking to the ugly old fir tree," said the child, and he trod upon the branches till they cracked again under his boots.

And the Tree looked at all the blooming flowers and the splendor of the garden, and then looked at itself, and wished it had remained in the dark corner of the garret. It thought of its fresh youth in the wood, of the merry Christmas Eve, and of the little Mice which had listened so pleasantly to the story of Klumpey-Dumpey.

"Past! past!" said the old Tree. "Had I but rejoiced when I could have done so! Past! past!"

And the servant came and chopped the Tree into little pieces; a whole bundle lay there. It blazed brightly under the great brewing copper, and it sighed deeply, and each sigh was like a little shot. And the children who were at play there ran up and seated themselves at the fire, looked into it, and cried, "Puff! Puff!" But at each explosion, which was a deep sigh, the tree thought of a summer day in the woods, or of a winter night there, when the stars beamed; he thought of Christmas Eve and of Klumpey-Dumpey, the only story he had ever heard or knew how to tell. And then the Tree was burned.

The boys played in the garden, and the youngest had on his breast a golden star, which the Tree had worn on its happiest evening. Now that was past, and the Tree's life was past, and the story is past too: Past! past!—and that's the way with all stories.

Gift of the Magi

O. HENRY

There was clearly nothing to do but flop down on the shabby little couch and howl. So Della did it. Which instigates the moral reflection that life is made up of sobs, sniffles, and smiles, with sniffles predominating. While the mistress of the home is gradually subsiding from the first stage to the second, take a look at the home. A furnished flat at $8 per week. It did not exactly beggar description, but it certainly had that word on the lookout for the mendicancy squad.

In the vestibule below was a letter-box into which no letter would go, and an electric button from which no mortal finger could coax a ring. Also appearing thereunto was a card bearing the name. "Mr. James Dillingham Young."

The "Dillingham" had been flung to the breeze during a former period of prosperity when its possessor was being paid $30 per week. Now, when the income was shrunk to $20, the letters of "Dillingham" looked blurred, as though they were thinking seriously of contracting to a modest and unassuming D. But whenever Mr. James Dillingham Young came home and reached his flat above he was called "Jim" and greatly hugged by Mrs. James Dillingham Young, already introduced to you as Della. Which is all very good.

Della finished her cry and attended to her cheeks with the powder rag. She stood by the window and looked out dully at a gray cat, walking a gray fence in a gray backyard. Tomorrow would be Christmas Day, and she had only $1.87 with which to buy Jim a present. She had been saving every penny she could for months, with this result. Twenty dollars a week doesn't go far. Expenses had been greater than she had calculated. They always are. Only $1.87 to buy a present for Jim. Her Jim. Many a happy hour she had spent planning for something nice for him. Something fine and rare and sterling—something just a little bit near to being worthy of the honor of being owned by Jim.

There was a pier-glass between the windows of the room. Perhaps you have seen a pier-glass in an $8 flat. A very thin and very agile person may, by observing his reflection in a rapid sequence of longitudinal strips, obtain a fairly accurate conception of his looks. Della, being slender, had mastered the art. Suddenly she whirled from the window and stood before the glass. Her eyes were shining brilliantly, but her face had lost its color within twenty seconds. Rapidly she pulled down her hair and let it fall to its full length.

Now, there were two possessions of the James Dillingham Youngs in which they both took a mighty pride. One was Jim's gold watch that had been his father's and his grandfather's. The other was Della's hair. Had the Queen of Sheba lived in the flat across the airshaft, Della would have let her hair hang out the window some day to dry just to depreciate Her Majesty's jewels and gifts. Had King Solomon been the janitor, with all his treasures piled up in the basement, Jim would have pulled out his watch every time he passed, just to see him pluck at his beard from envy.

So now Della's beautiful hair fell about her rippling and shining like a cascade of brown waters. It reached below her knee and made itself almost a garment for her. And then she did it up again nervously and quickly. Once she faltered for a minute and stood still while a tear or two splashed on the worn red carpet.

On went her old brown jacket; on went her old brown hat. With a whirl of skirts and with the brilliant sparkle still in her eyes, she fluttered out the door and down the stairs to the street.

Where she stopped the sign read: "Mme. Sofronie. Hair Goods of All Kinds." One flight up Della ran, and collected herself, panting. Madame, large, too white, chilly, hardly looked the "Sofronie."

Will you buy my hair?" asked Della.

"I buy hair," said Madame. "Take yer hat off and let's have a sight at the looks of it."

Down rippled the brown cascade. "Twenty dollars," said Madame, lifting the mass with a practiced hand.

"Give it to me quick," said Della.

Oh, and the next two hours tripped by on rosy wings. Forget the hashed metaphor. She was ransacking the stores for Jim's present. She found it at last. It surely had been made for Jim and no one else. There was no other like it in any of the stores, and she had turned all of them inside out. It was a platinum fob chain simple and chaste in design, properly proclaiming its value by substance alone and not by meretricious ornamentation—as all good things should do. It was even worthy of The Watch. As soon as she saw it she knew that it must be Jim's. It was like him. Quietness and value—the description applied to both. Twenty-one dollars they took from her for it, and she hurried home with the 87 cents. With that chain on his watch Jim might be properly anxious about the time in any company. Grand as the watch was, he sometimes looked at it on the sly on account of the old leather strap that he used in place of a chain.

When Della reached home her intoxication gave way a little to prudence and reason. She got out her curling irons and lighted the gas and went to work repairing the ravages made by generosity added to love. Which is always a tremendous task, dear friends—a mammoth task.

Within forty minutes her head was covered with tiny, close-lying curls that made her look wonderfully like a truant schoolboy. She looked at her reflection in the mirror long, carefully, and critically.

"If Jim doesn't kill me." she said to herself, "before he takes a second look at me, he'll say I look like a Coney Island chorus girl. But what could I do—oh! What could I do with a dollar and eighty-seven cents?"

At 7 o'clock the coffee was made and the frying-pan was on the back of the stove hot and ready to cook the chops.

Jim was never late. Della doubled the fob chain in her hand and sat on the corner of the table near the door that he always entered. Then she heard his step on the stair way down on the first flight, and she turned white for just a moment. She had a habit of saying little silent prayers about the simplest everyday things and now she whispered: "Please God, make him think I am still pretty."

The door opened and Jim stepped in and closed it. He looked thin and very serious. Poor fellow, he was only twenty-two—and to be burdened with a family! He needed a new overcoat and he was without gloves.

Jim stopped inside the door, as immovable as a setter at the scent of quail. His eyes were fixed upon Della, and there was an expression in them that she could not read, and it terrified her. It was not anger, nor surprise, nor disapproval, nor horror, nor any of the sentiments that she had been prepared for. He simply stared at her fixedly with that peculiar expression on his face.

Della wriggled off the table and went for him.

"Jim, darling," she cried, "don't look at me that way. I had my hair cut off and sold it because I couldn't have lived through Christmas without giving you a present. It'll grow out again—you won't mind, will you? I just had to do it. My hair grows awfully fast. Say 'Merry Christmas!' Jim, and let's be happy. You don't know what a nice—what a beautiful, nice gift I've got for you."

"You've cut off your hair?" asked Jim, laboriously, as if he had not arrived at that patent fact yet even after the hardest mental labor.

"Cut it off and sold it," said Della. "Don't you like me just as well, anyhow? I'm me without my hair, ain't I?"

Jim looked about the room curiously.

"You say your hair is gone?" he said, with an air almost of idiocy.

"You needn't look for it," said Della. "It's sold, I tell you—sold and gone, too. It's Christmas Eve, boy. Be good to me, for it went for you. Maybe the hairs of my head were numbered," she went on with a sudden serious sweetness, "but nobody could ever count my love for you. Shall I put the chops on, Jim?"

Out of his trance Jim seemed quickly to wake. He enfolded his Della. For ten seconds let us regard with discreet scrutiny some inconsequential object in the other direction. Eight dollars a week or a million a year—what is the difference? A mathematician or a wit would give you the wrong answer. The magi brought valuable gifts, but that was not among them. This dark assertion will be illuminated later on.

Jim drew a package from his overcoat pocket and threw it upon the table.

"Don't make any mistake, Dell," he said, "about me. I don't think there's anything in the way of a haircut or a shave or a shampoo that could make me like my girl any less. But if you'll unwrap that package you may see why you had me going a while at first."

White fingers and nimble tore at the string and paper. And then an ecstatic scream of joy; and then, alas! a quick feminine change to hysterical tears and wails, necessitating the immediate employment of all the comforting powers of the lord of the flat.

For there lay The Combs—the set of combs, side and back, that Della had worshipped for long in a Broadway window. Beautiful combs, pure tortoise shell, with jewelled rims—just the shade to wear in the beautiful vanished hair. They were expensive combs, she knew, and her heart had simply craved and yearned over them without the least hope of possession. And now, they were hers, but the tresses that should have adorned the coveted adornments were gone.

But she hugged them to her bosom, and at length she was able to look up with dim eyes and a smile and say: "My hair grows so fast, Jim!"

And then Della leaped up like a little singed cat and cried, "Oh, oh!"

Jim had not yet seen his beautiful present. She held it out to him eagerly upon her open palm. The dull precious metal seemed to flash with a reflection of her bright and ardent spirit.

"Isn't it a dandy, Jim? I hunted all over town to find it. You'll have to look at the time a hundred times a day now. Give me your watch. I want to see how it looks on it."

Instead of obeying, Jim tumbled down on the couch and put his hands under the back of his head and smiled.

"Dell," said he, "let's put our Christmas presents away and keep 'em a while. They're too nice to use just at present. I sold the watch to get the money to buy your combs. And now suppose you put the chops on."

The magi, as you know, were wise men—wonderfully wise men—who brought gifts to the Babe in the manger. They invented the art of giving Christmas presents. Being wise, their gifts were no doubt wise ones, possibly bearing the privilege of exchange in case of duplication. And here I have lamely related to you the uneventful chronicle of two foolish children in a flat who most unwisely sacrificed for each other the greatest treasures of their house. But in a last word to the wise of these days let it be said that of all who give gifts these two were the wisest. Of all who give and receive gifts, such as they are wisest. Everywhere they are wisest. They are the magi.

———————— ✳ ————————

The Night Before Christmas

CLEMENT C. MOORE

'Twas the night before Christmas,
　　　when all through the house
Not a creature was stirring,
　　　not even a mouse;
The stockings were hung by the chimney with care,
In hopes that St. Nicholas soon would be there;
The children were nestled all snug in their beds,
While visions of sugarplums danced in their heads;

And Mamma in her 'kerchief, and I in my cap,
Had just settled our brains for a long winter's nap;
When out on the lawn there arose such a clatter,
I sprang from the bed to see what was the matter.
Away to the window I flew like a flash,
Tore open the shutters and threw up the sash.

The moon, on the breast of the new-fallen snow,
Gave the lustre of midday to objects below,
When what to my wondering eyes should appear,
But a miniature sleigh, and eight tiny reindeer,
With a little old driver, so lively and quick,
I knew in a moment it must be St. Nick.

More rapid than eagles his coursers they came,
And he whistled and shouted, and called them by name;
'Now, Dasher! Now, Dancer! Now, Prancer and Vixen!
On, Comet! On, Cupid! On, Donner and Blitzen!
To the top of the porch! To the top of the wall!
Now, dash away! Dash away! Dash away all!'

As dry leaves that before the wild hurricane fly,
When they meet with an obstacle, mount to the sky;
So up to the housetop the coursers they flew,
With the sleigh full of toys, and St. Nicholas, too.

And then, in a twinkling, I heard on the roof
The prancing and pawing of each little hoof—
As I drew in my head, and was turning around,
Down the chimney St. Nicholas came with a bound.

He was dressed all in fur, from his head to his foot,
And his clothes were all tarnished with ashes and soot;
A bundle of toys he had flung on his back,
And he looked like a pedlar just opening his pack.
His eyes—how they twinkled! His dimples, how merry!
His cheeks were like roses, his nose like a cherry!

His droll little mouth was drawn up like a bow,
And the beard of his chin was as white as the snow;
The stump of a pipe he held tight in his teeth,
And the smoke it encircled his head like a wreath;
He had a broad face and a little round belly
That shook, when he laughed, like a bowl
        full of jelly.

He was chubby and plump, a right jolly
        old elf,
And I laughed, when I saw him, in spite
        of myself;
A wink of his eye and a twist of his head,
Soon gave me to know I had nothing
        to dread;
He spoke not a word, but went straight
        to his work,
And filled all the stockings; then turned
        with a jerk,

And laying his finger aside
        of his nose,
And giving a nod, up the
        chimney he rose;
He sprang to his sleigh, to his
        team gave a whistle,
And away they all flew like
        the down of a thistle.
But I heard him exclaim, ere
        he drove out of sight,
'Happy Christmas to all,
        and to all a good night.'

The Christmas Heretic

J. EDGAR PARK

Our street, like your street, might have been considered humdrum and ordinary. The usual folks lived in the usual houses. We got up about the same time and went to work about the same time and went to bed about half past ten—or our neighbors knew the reason why.

But there is a fantastic world just a millionth of an inch below the surface of the regular world. The only thing you really know about life is—that you never can tell. A new personality may drop into the most ordinary street and disturb the even surface with strange impossibilities. That is what happened on our street.

We were all away the day the Joneses moved in. Have you ever heard of anyone's moving on Thanksgiving Day? We never had. When we got home from Grandfather's the next morning we were astonished to see burlap and excelsior around the doors of No. 17. The draperies were up in the parlor. They must have got settled very quickly.

As I passed on my way to work, the remover's man, who evidently had stayed after the vans had left and who looked as if he had been working all night, was gathering up the remains of a broken chair or two that lay at the gate. He was very angry and tired, and was communicating some of his wrath to our genial street cleaner, Tony, who was always on hand to make friends with everybody.

"I'll never move for him again!" he was saying as I passed. "Of all the bad-tempered cusses I ever met, he is the absolute limit, scolding and fussing all day. I never did hear such language, over a few broken chairs and crockery and such like!"

Just then a man, whom I afterward discovered to be Mr. Jones, came down the steps radiant with smiles and good humor, and placing a bill in the hands of the astonished man said, "That's for yourself! And a thousand thanks for all your care and work!" It was a strange sight, the disgruntled man just halted in his imprecations, gazing at a bill whose proportions evidently astounded him, and Mr. Jones with hearty hand outstretched to say good-bye. Then the corner of the house hid them from my view, an incredible tableau.

Few people could win their way into the esteem of their neighbors as quickly as did Mr. Jones. He was the friend of every child on the street before he had been with us a week. Inside a month every boy in the vicinity had been allowed to work the wireless he had fitted up in his attic. His predecessor had been so bothered by children's riding their bicycles over his walks—for there was a lovely turn around the house—that he had put up a bit of barbed wire and a notice: "Children Keep Off. Police Take Notice." Mr. Jones took down the wire and taught one of our little girls how to ride round, coasting the last part of the way. He used the notice to fill up a cross drain so that the children could ride more smoothly. Our new neighbor proved to be an artist in the planning of the most satisfactory surprises. He always had an extra ticket for a ball game, an extra seat or two in his car when going for a ride.

Yet Mr. Jones was not to be explained simply as a kind-hearted man. There were complications. The remarks of the furniture remover lingered in my mind as an inexplicable mystery. And on Christmas Day I was reminded of that curious scene at his gate.

This newcomer had become such a favorite with us all that we vied with one another as to who should have the pleasure of entertaining him on Christmas Day. We found that he had had six invitations from our street alone. I will not conceal the fact that in three of these houses there were marriageable daughters—for Mr. Jones was a bachelor; but I think he would have been invited anyway. Each of us felt sure our new neighbor would come to us, for to each of us he had become so special and personal a friend that it had not struck us that he could seem so much a part of any other family as he did of ours. All the invitations he refused. We were surprised, and I confess the idea occurred to me that perhaps he was preparing some special surprise for the children on that day.

The children in our house were all up on Christmas morning at crack of dawn and rushed down at once to investigate the contents of their stockings. Mildred was overjoyed with her presents; but after going all over them twice she returned to her stocking again. Something troubled the child, I could see. Finding it really empty, she turned to her brother George and asked, "Did you get a present from Mr. Jones, George?" "No, that's funny, I didn't," he said. Somehow, Mr. Jones seemed to our children such a familiar friend that they had expected to be remembered by him. They had had great fun in preparing the little gifts they had dropped into his letter box, the evening before.

After the stocking presents had been admired and exhibited, it was still a long time till breakfast, and Mildred suggested they go out for a spin on their wheels, for it was sunny, snowless and mild. In ten minutes Mildred was back again, with indignant tears on her cheeks, and George scared and sobbing. They could hardly tell their story for emotion. They had been having a lovely time cycling about that beautiful turn around Mr. Jones's house. Mildred confessed that she had been going so fast that her wheel had gone off the asphalt walk onto the lawn; but she had often had the same experience before when Mr. Jones was teaching her.

This time, however, the window had opened and Mr. Jones had put his head out and had scolded them both terribly. How in the world, he said, could he keep a lawn looking like anything with all the kids in the street riding their wheels all over the grass. Give people an inch and they'll take an ell! If people cannot train their children to behave properly he wished they'd keep them at home! These were some of the remarks Mildred and George remembered and told us amid their sobs. I was incredulous till I looked out the window and saw Mr. Jones in his dressing gown, struggling with a tangle of barbed wire. He had put the notice back just where the Browns had had it, and was now fixing up the wire again. Some neighbors' boys, who went to his house for some fun with the wireless later, were, to their astonishment and indignation, thrown out, on the ground that they had dirtied the stair carpets with their muddy boots and had several times come in without permission at all.

The only explanation that we could find for Mr. Jones's behavior that evening at our Neighborhood Club Christmas Dance was that he must have been under the influence of liquor. Miss Farquerson left early, in tears. When I was going away after a heated political discussion into which he had drawn me unawares, and in which he had told me just what he thought of our popular local representative, I heard his voice, loud and rasping, informing Mrs. Francis Nosegood, "You folks in this neighborhood live in a puddle and think it is the world!"

It seemed, that evening, as we all retired for the night, that in no home in the street could Mr. Jones ever be forgiven. And yet, as I have indicated, his charm and goodness of heart, which asserted themselves again next morning, were so genuine that, in my mind at least, the experience of Christmas Day, like the remarks of the furniture remover, sank into the background of my consciousness as an inexplicable mystery. Next morning he took the wire and the notice down again and he re-won the affection of Mildred and George by a series of remarkably adroit and flattering attentions and kindnesses.

Mrs. Francis Nosegood, however, did not seem able to forgive him. She was the lady who lived in the

big house at the corner. She had decided opinions. We were all familiar with her simple philosophy of life. People were either good or bad. Most people were at heart bad. They pretended to be good and often were able to deceive others for a time. But, sooner or later, to a shrewd observer like Mrs. Nosegood, they gave themselves away. Mr. Jones had given himself away. It remained for Mrs. Nosegood to follow up the clue and prove that his remark about the mud puddle was no mere accidental observation but a clear symptom of deep-seated moral depravity. It became her duty to expose his hypocrisy.

She despised us all for allowing Mr. Jones to "bribe" us into liking him again by what she called his "puny charities." Having nothing to do, she was immediately hot upon the scent of his past. We saw her coming out of the real-estate office with a triumphant air; she had a confidential interview with the mail carrier; she happened to pass just as Mr. Jones's housekeeper was going out shopping, and walked down town with her. Soon she began to wear an air of secret and invincible power whenever she haughtily acknowledged his greeting.

Meanwhile, Mr. Jones, seemingly in quiet unconsciousness of his new enemy, continued to act the part of Providence in our street, kind to just and unjust, naughty and good alike, with a sort of omnipotent casualness. He visited and entertained us all till he was to each of us a personal friend.

In a month or so Mrs. Nosegood left for a short visit in Manchester, New Hampshire. It seems the real-estate man had told her he understood Mr. Jones had moved here from that city. Mr. Jones, however, heard of her destination without any apparent uneasiness. She was gone for the better part of a week and returned triumphant. The next evening she called on us immediately after dinner. Her suspicions had been confirmed. On the twenty-ninth of February she had made her great discovery,—that Mr. Jones had lived in the outskirts of Manchester with an old aunt who had brought him up since childhood. His violent bursts of temper had become notorious among the neighbors, and it was generally understood that relations between him and his wealthy old aunt were very unhappy at times, owing to these sudden fits of ungovernable rage. One day, the old aunt, who had been shopping all the afternoon, returned home in the best of health. According to his story, she was on her way upstairs when he heard her fall. Rushing up from the cellar where he was, he said, sorting apples, he found her lying in the hallway—dead. There was great indignation among the neighbors when this story became known; an inquiry was instituted and much testimony was heard; he was committed for trial, but in the end the jury disagreed and he was acquitted. Popular indignation, however, ran so high that he had to leave Manchester and, till Mrs. Nosegood's arrival, his whereabouts had been unknown. Mrs. Nosegood had talked on that day with many of the neighbors and had found that in Manchester Mr. Jones had evinced no special interest in children or neighbors. It was evident, she pointed out, that these traits were simply assumed here, as she had suspected all along, as a mere hypocritical screen.

The subject of her investigations happened to drop in before she left, and she took occasion to say to him in the most pointed manner, "I met some of your old acquaintances, Mr. Jones, in Manchester, these last few days."

"Well, well," he said, beaming on her in the most unconscious way in the world. "I didn't know I had any friends up there. Who were they, may I ask?"

"I met the Thompsons and the Blythes," she answered. As she afterward told us, these were the two nearest neighbors to the house where Mr. Jones had lived.

She spoke with such a meaning stare that he seemed disconcerted and passed it off with "Well, I hope they gave a good account of me, anyway!" Then he gaily changed the subject, and in a few moments Mrs. Nosegood, almost speechless with indignation, went away.

With incredible ingenuity Mrs. Nosegood now began to dig the pit beneath the unsuspecting feet of Mr. Jones. When Mr. Jones was absent her arguments were so cogent that we were almost convinced; but I confess all of them faded into thin air in the genial and kindly presence of that gentleman himself. All summer long Mrs. Nosegood sat in the window behind the curtain and watched the Jones house whenever Mr. Jones was at home. She went away for a well-earned vacation only after she had seen him off for his.

In the fall, a chemical laboratory in one of the upper rooms of the Jones house was added to the wireless equipment—as a further attraction to the boys of the neighborhood. Mr. Jones was a scientific expert of some kind in a large manufacturing concern and, according to the boys, was experimenting till late into the night with certain rare and deadly chemicals. This gave Mrs. Nosegood her next clue. It was now clear that the rich old aunt had been poisoned.

Thanksgiving Day came, the first anniversary of Mr. Jones's arrival. As usual, we went away the evening before to Grandfather's farm. When we returned the morning after Thanksgiving Day we heard of strange doings in our absence. It seemed that Mr. Jones had chosen that day in which to do his "spring cleaning." He had got two Polish girls to assist his housekeeper, and through the open windows could be heard the storming, growling voice of Mr. Jones, scolding and complaining at the poor women as they worked. This went on, the neighbors said, all day, till at six o'clock he let the girls go.

At the Thanksgiving reception at the Neighborhood Club, on the evening of Thanksgiving Day, he had insisted on relating to the whole company his troubles—the clumsy women, the way they had disarranged his books and instruments with bottomless stupidity. He vented his spleen on the whole company, complaining on the general incapacity of every one.

At this, Miss Farquerson, the pretty one from the house opposite, being a college girl and knowing her own mind, could stand it no longer, and told him just what she thought of him. The girl's genuine wrath became her very well. He stopped and looked at her fixedly for a moment, and then said, "Bah! The more I see of people the more thankful I am that my special investigation at this time is the various uses of arsenic!"

At this word, they told us, Mrs. Nosegood looked around triumphantly. Within a week she was back in Manchester, New Hampshire. She told the Thompsons and the Blythes of her further evidence. They put their heads together, and with the consent of the new tenant of the Jones house they made a thorough investigation of the house from cellar to attic. There were no results; but the apple closet in the cellar was locked and the key in the pocket of the owner, who happened to be away from home. The Blythes promised to investigate that closet as soon as he returned. Mrs. Nosegood came back to her armchair at the window, from which she kept track of every movement of Mr. Jones. He was friendly with every household on the street except her own and Miss Farquerson's, whom he apparently had never forgiven for her frank speech on Thanksgiving Day. Mrs. Nosegood rejoiced in this and missed no opportunity to bestow favors on that young lady, especially in the presence of Mr. Jones.

Christmas Day came again. Christmas trees or Christmas turkeys came to every door on the street except that of Mr. Jones. Early in the morning of Christmas Day he apparently came down and closed his dog outside his door and let him howl horribly there the rest of the hours of darkness, keeping all his neighbors awake. He made his housekeeper wash after breakfast and hung the entire wash out with his own hands, not, as usually, in the screened place behind the house, but on a rope tied between two trees on the front lawn. He then brought out his ash barrels, which the city teams were to call for next day, and put them in a row—he must have been saving them for the purpose for weeks—on the sidewalk in front of his house. Thus he effectively spoiled the looks of the street and gave a black eye to the whole neighborhood. He then resurrected from somewhere a horrible gramophone and, placing it at an open window, ground out on it over and over again the cheapest and most exasperating records he could find. At dinner hour he came out of the house, kicked the dog into howling again, and, making deep-track short cuts over all our lawns and flower beds, disappeared for a walk—thus giving Mrs. Nosegood a chance to go down from her watchtower for her dinner.

The usual Christmas Festival was held at our little Neighborhood Club that evening. We were all with Mrs. Nosegood now, heartily angry with Mr. Jones; we avoided him when he arrived. Mrs. Nosegood came in late and, beckoning to me, told me in tremendous excitement that she had just had a telegram from Manchester, New Hampshire, absolutely establishing Mr. Jones's guilt. He had poisoned his wealthy aunt with arsenic. She had a telegram from the Blythes saying that they had just discovered, under a barrel of rotten apples in the cellar closet, four papers full of a white powder and labeled "Arsenic."

Around the supper table we usually had speeches and toasts of a friendly and amusing nature. The laughter after one of these had died down when I discovered, to my astonishment, Mr. Jones upon his feet. He was about to make a speech. Mrs. Nosegood clutched at her telegram and looked at him with triumphant disdain.

"Friends," he began, "this is a great day in my life, and I am going to ask you to permit me to tell you a little about myself, if it will not bore you." There being no particular dissent, if no great enthusiasm, Mr. Jones continued: "It may surprise you to know that I lived, before arriving here, in Manchester, New Hampshire."

At this, Mrs. Nosegood, unable to contain herself any longer, leapt to her feet and with blazing eye cried out: "Mr. Jones, it may surprise you to know that we know a great deal more about you than you think. I have here in my hand a telegram establishing your guilt. Mr. Jones, your aunt did not die as a result of falling downstairs. She died as a result of arsenic poisoning and you were the murderer." With this she handed the telegram to Mr. Jones.

He read it twice and laid it down, with calmness, at his plate. "I have been guilty, very guilty in this matter, I confess," he said, "but to-night I am going to make a full confession to you all."

The old spell of his friendly courtesy seemed to be weaving itself around us once more. Mrs. Nosegood appealed to Miss Farquerson that he be not heard. But Miss Farquerson quietly answered, "I think it only fair to hear his side of the case, if he has one."

Mr. Jones, with simplicity, continued: "It evidently does not surprise you to know that before I came here I lived in Manchester, New Hampshire. The people among whom I lived were ordinary people; that is to say, they acted as if it were natural to be selfish, and as if there must be a special reason or a special occasion for any act of public spirit or good will. So, while living all the year as selfish lookers-after-themselves, they were terrible sentimentalists about Christmas and Thanksgiving. On these days they dabbled in a little amateurish way at those concerns which ought to have been the main business of their lives—true friendliness and neighborliness.

"After a while I found two homes in Manchester where there were friends who agreed with my point of view, and in process of time we came to live in three houses next one another—the Thompsons, the Blythes, and I. We formed a club founded upon our principles, and I should like to read you the constitution of that club." He took up a small piece of paper and read:

PRINCIPLES OF THE THREE HUNDRED AND SIXTY-THREE CLUB

1. Every one ought to be generous and thankful every day in the year.
2. Nobody can be generous and thankful every day in the year.
3. Therefore, be it enacted, that we, the members of this club, do observe as solemn festivals two days in every year, (a) The National Day of Grumbling and Growling, and (b) Devilmas Day. Into the first of these we shall try to concentrate all the necessary grumbling and growling which has to be indulged in by any decent man who is human. On it we shall try to locate those tasks (like moving or house cleaning) which cannot be accomplished by any one not a hypocrite, without tension, strain, and profanity. And on Devilmas Day we shall try to work off all the year's

accumulated meanness which, even in the best of lives, must accumulate, and even by the best of men must somehow be worked off, if insanity is to be dodged. The rest of the three hundred and sixty-three days of the year we shall observe as Thanksgiving and Christmas Days.

"We lived for some years to our own great satisfaction and, I fear, to the utter mystification of our neighbors, in obedience to these principles. Then business changes made it necessary for me to move away.

"Last year I observed Devilmas Day, as you may remember, on the 25th day of December by working off some of my accumulated irritation at the rudeness and carelessness of some of your children. This, together with my extremely irritated remark to Mrs. Nosegood, made me sure that a woman of her type would try to prove, from my past, her theory about me.

"My last action last Devilmas Day was to write to my friends, the Thompsons and Blythes, in Manchester, to tell them that an old woman named Nosegood would be there soon to look up my record. I told them to tell her I was suspected of killing my aunt. My aunt never really existed. I should not be so queer, perhaps, if I were not an only child of two only children.

"This telegram which I hold shows me that my friends in Manchester, true to their vows, are celebrating Devilmas Day in their own jovial fashion. My friends, I call you to witness that my celebration of these festivals has been just a concentration at my house of things that do happen elsewhere in our street all through the year."

We hung our heads, as one of us was guilty of premature ash barrels, one of an occasional public wash, and another of the nocturnal howling dog.

"My friends," he continued, "I was wrong. I am here to confess it heartily and to ask your pardon. Once a man ceases being a mere observer and becomes really entangled in life, he needs far more of an outlet for growling and devilment than I had supposed. I hereby renounce my previous plan and return with the rest of you to the method of trying to be as nice as possible two days in the year."

Turning to Mrs. Nosegood he continued: "It may astonish you to learn that right here under your eyes and without your knowledge has taken place one of the most thrilling of modern dramas. A would-be onlooker in your street has been entangled in life by love; or, to put the matter in a more conventional way, Miss Farquerson and I have the honor to announce—"

When, after a few moments, Doctor Brown returned to the table and said that Mrs. Nosegood had recovered so far that he thought it was all right to send her home in the station hack, Mr. Jones came round and took the place she had so suddenly vacated beside Miss Farquerson.

The Peterkins' Christmas-Tree

---※---

LUCRETIA P. HALE

*E*arly in the autumn the Peterkins began to prepare for their Christmas-tree. Everything was done in great privacy, as it was to be a surprise to the neighbors, as well as to the rest of the family. Mr. Peterkin had been up to Mr. Bromwick's woodlot, and with his consent, selected the tree. Agamemnon went to look at it occasionally after dark, and Solomon John made frequent visits to it mornings, just after sunrise. Mr. Peterkin drove Elizabeth Eliza and her mother that way, and pointed furtively to it with his whip; but none of them ever spoke of it aloud to each other. It was suspected that the little boys had been to see it Wednesday and Saturday afternoons. But they came home with their pockets full of chestnuts, and said nothing about it.

At length Mr. Peterkin had it cut down and brought secretly into the Larkins' barn. A week or two before Christmas a measurement was made of it with Elizabeth Eliza's yard-measure. To Mr. Peterkin's great dismay it was discovered that it was too high to stand in the back parlor.

This fact was brought out at a secret council of Mr. and Mrs. Peterkin, Elizabeth Eliza, and Agamemnon.

Agamemnon suggested that it might be set up slanting; but Mrs. Peterkin was very sure it would make her dizzy, and the candles would drip.

But a brilliant idea came to Mr. Peterkin. He proposed that the ceiling of the parlor should be raised to make room for the top of the tree.

Elizabeth Eliza thought the space would need to be quite large. It must not be like a small box, or you could not see the tree.

"Yes," said Mr. Peterkin, "I should have the ceiling lifted all across the room; the effect would be finer."

Elizabeth Eliza objected to having the whole ceiling raised, because her room was over the back parlor, and she would have no floor while the alteration was going on, which would be very awkward. Besides, her room was not very high now, and, if the floor were raised, perhaps she could not walk in it upright.

Mr. Peterkin explained that he didn't propose altering the whole ceiling, but to lift up a ridge across the room at the back part where the tree was to stand. This would make a hump, to be sure, in Elizabeth Eliza's room; but it would go across the whole room.

Elizabeth Eliza said she would not mind that. It would be like the cuddy thing that comes up on the deck of a ship, that you sit against, only here you would not have the sea-sickness. She thought she should like it, for a rarity. She might use it for a divan.

Mrs. Peterkin thought it would come in the worn place of the carpet, and might be a convenience in making the carpet over.

Agamemnon was afraid there would be trouble in keeping the matter secret, for it would be a long piece of work for a carpenter; but Mr. Peterkin proposed having the carpenter for a day or two, for a number of other jobs.

One of them was to make all the chairs in the house of the same height, for Mrs. Peterkin had nearly broken her spine by sitting down in a chair that she had supposed was her own rocking-chair, and it had proved to be two inches lower. The little boys were now large enough to sit in any chair; so a medium was fixed upon to satisfy all the family, and the chairs were made uniformly of the same height.

On consulting the carpenter, however, he insisted that the tree could be cut off at the lower end to suit the height of the parlor, and demurred at so great a change as altering the ceiling. But Mr. Peterkin had set his mind upon the improvement, and Elizabeth Eliza had cut her carpet in preparation for it.

So the folding-doors into the back parlor were closed, and for nearly a fortnight before Christmas there was great litter of fallen plastering, and laths, and chips, and shavings; and Elizabeth Eliza's carpet was taken up, and the furniture had to be changed, and one night she had to sleep at the Bromwicks', for there was a long hole in her floor that might be dangerous.

All this delighted the little boys. They could not understand what was going on. Perhaps they suspected a Christmas-tree, but they did not know why a Christmas-tree should have so many chips, and were still more astonished at the hump that appeared in Elizabeth Eliza's room. It must be a Christmas present, or else the tree in a box.

Some aunts and uncles, too, arrived a day or two before Christmas, with some small cousins. These cousins occupied the attention of the little boys, and there was a great deal of whispering and mystery, behind doors, and under the stairs, and in the corners of the entry.

Solomon John was busy, privately making some candles for the tree. He had been collecting some bayberries, as he understood they made very nice candles, so that it would not be necessary to buy any.

The elders of the family never all went into the back parlor together, and all tried not to see what was going on. Mrs. Peterkin would go in with Solomon John, or Mr. Peterkin with Elizabeth Eliza, or Elizabeth Eliza and Agamemnon and Solomon John. The little boys and the small cousins were never allowed even to look inside the room.

Elizabeth Eliza meanwhile went into town a number of times. She wanted to consult Amanda as to how much ice-cream they should need, and whether they could make it at home, as they had cream and ice. She was pretty busy in her own room; the furniture had to be changed, and the carpet altered. The "hump" was higher than she expected. There was danger of bumping her own head whenever she crossed it. She had to nail some padding on the ceiling for fear of accidents.

The afternoon before Christmas, Elizabeth Eliza, Solomon John, and their father collected in the back parlor for a council. The carpenters had done their work, and the tree stood at its full height at the back of the room, the top stretching up into the space arranged for it. All the chips and shavings were cleared away, and it stood on a neat box.

But what were they to put upon the tree?

Solomon John had brought in his supply of candles; but they proved to be very "stringy" and very few of them. It was strange how many bayberries it took to make a few candles! The little boys had helped him, and he had gathered as much as a bushel of bayberries. He had put them in water, and skimmed off the wax, according to the directions; but there was so little wax!

Solomon John had given the little boys some of the bits sawed off from the legs of the chairs. He had suggested that they should cover them with gilt paper, to answer for gilt apples, without telling them what they were for.

These apples, a little blunt at the end, and the candles, were all they had for the tree!

After all her trips into town Elizabeth Eliza had forgotten to bring anything for it.

"I thought of candies and sugar-plums," she said; "but I concluded if we made caramels ourselves we

should not need them. But, then, we have not made caramels. The fact is, that day my head was full of my carpet. I had bumped it pretty badly, too."

Mr. Peterkin wished he had taken, instead of a fir-tree, an apple-tree he had seen in October, full of red fruit.

"But the leaves would have fallen off by this time," said Elizabeth Eliza.

"And the apples, too," said Solomon John.

"It is odd I should have forgotten, that day I went in on purpose to get the things," said Elizabeth Eliza, musingly. "But I went from shop to shop, and didn't know exactly what to get. I saw a great many gilt things for Christmas-trees; but I knew the little boys were making the gilt apples; there were plenty of candles in the shops, but I knew Solomon John was making the candles."

Mr. Peterkin thought it was quite natural.

Solomon John wondered if it were too late for them to go into town now.

Elizabeth Eliza could not go in the next morning, for there was to be a grand Christmas dinner, and

Mr. Peterkin could not be spared, and Solomon John was sure he and Agamemnon would not know what to buy. Besides, they would want to try the candles to-night.

Mr. Peterkin asked if the presents everybody had been preparing would not answer. But Elizabeth Eliza knew they would be too heavy.

A gloom came over the room. There was only a flickering gleam from one of Solomon John's candles that he had lighted by way of trial.

Solomon John again proposed going into town. He lighted a match to examine the newspaper about the trains. There were plenty of trains coming out at that hour, but none going in except a very late one. That would not leave time to do anything and come back.

"We could go in, Elizabeth Eliza and I," said Solomon John, "but we should not have time to buy anything."

Agamemnon was summoned in. Mrs. Peterkin was entertaining the uncles and aunts in the front parlor. Agamemnon wished there was time to study up something about electric lights. If they could only have a calcium light! Solomon John's candle sputtered and went out.

At this moment there was a loud knocking at the front door. The little boys, and the small cousins, and the uncles and aunts, and Mrs. Peterkin, hastened to see what was the matter.

The uncles and aunts thought somebody's house must be on fire. The door was opened, and there was a man, white with flakes, for it was beginning to snow, and he was pulling in a large box.

Mrs. Peterkin supposed it contained some of Elizabeth Eliza's purchases, so she ordered it to be pushed into the back parlor, and hastily called back her guests and the little boys into the other room. The little boys and the small cousins were sure they had seen Santa Claus himself.

Mr. Peterkin lighted the gas. The box was addressed to Elizabeth Eliza. It was from the lady from Philadelphia! She had gathered a hint from Elizabeth Eliza's letters that there was to be a Christmas-tree, and had filled this box with all that would be needed.

It was opened directly. There was every kind of gilt hanging-thing, from gilt pea-pods to butterflies on springs. There were shining flags and lanterns, and bird-cages, and nests with birds sitting on them, baskets of fruit, gilt apples and bunches of grapes, and, at the bottom of the whole, a large box of candles and a box of Philadelphia bonbons!

Elizabeth Eliza and Solomon John could scarcely keep from screaming. The little boys and the small cousins knocked on the folding-doors to ask what was the matter.

Hastily Mr. Peterkin and the rest took out the things and hung them on the tree, and put on the candles.

When all was done, it looked so well that Mr. Peterkin exclaimed:—

"Let us light the candles now, and send to invite all the neighbors to-night, and have the tree on Christmas Eve!"

And so it was that the Peterkins had their Christmas-tree the day before, and on Christmas night could go and visit their neighbors.

from *The Peterkin Papers*

Bob Cratchit's Christmas

CHARLES DICKENS

Then up rose Mrs. Cratchit, Cratchit's wife, dressed out but poorly in a twice-turned gown, but brave in ribbons, which are cheap and make a goodly show for sixpence; and she laid the cloth, assisted by Belinda Cratchit, second of her daughters, also brave in ribbons; while Master Peter Cratchit plunged a fork into the saucepan of potatoes, and getting the corners of his monstrous shirt collar (Bob's private property, conferred upon his son and heir in honor of the day) into his mouth, rejoiced to find himself so gallantly attired, and yearned to show his linen in the fashionable Parks. And now two smaller Cratchits, boy and girl, came tearing in, screaming that outside the baker's they had smelt the goose, and known it for their own; and basking in luxurious thoughts of sage and onion, these young Cratchits danced about the table, and exalted Master Peter Cratchit to the skies, while he (not proud, although his collars nearly choked him) blew the fire, until the slow potatoes bubbling up, knocked loudly at the saucepan lid to be let out and peeled.

"What has ever got your precious father then?" said Mrs. Cratchit. "And your brother, Tiny Tim! And Martha warn't as late last Christmas Day by half-an-hour!"

"Here's Martha, Mother!" said a girl, appearing as she spoke.

"Here's Martha, Mother!" cried the two young Cratchits. "Hurrah! There's *such* a goose, Martha!"

"Why, bless your heart alive, my dear, how late you are!" said Mrs. Cratchit, kissing her a dozen times, and taking off her shawl and bonnet for her with officious zeal.

"We'd a deal of work to finish up last night," replied the girl, "and had to clear away this morning, Mother!"

"Well! Never mind so long as you are come," said Mrs. Cratchit. "Sit ye down before the fire, my dear, and have a warm, Lord bless ye!"

"No, no! There's Father coming!" cried the two young Cratchits, who were everywhere at once. "Hide, Martha, hide!"

So Martha hid herself, and in came little Bob, the father, with at least three feet of comforter exclusive of the fringe, hanging down before him; and his threadbare clothes darned up and brushed, to look seasonable; and Tiny Tim upon his shoulder. Alas for Tiny Tim, he bore a little crutch, and had his limbs supported by an iron frame!

"Why, where's our Martha?" cried Bob Cratchit, looking round.

"Not coming," said Mrs. Cratchit.

"Not coming!" said Bob, with a sudden declension in his high spirits; for he had been Tom's blood horse all the way from church, and had come home rampant. "Not coming upon Christmas Day!"

Martha didn't like to see him disappointed, if it were only in joke; so she came out prematurely from behind the closet door, and ran into his arms, while the two young Cratchits hustled Tiny Tim, and bore him off into the wash-house, that he might hear the pudding singing in the copper.

"And how did little Tim behave?" asked Mrs. Cratchit, when she had rallied Bob on his credulity, and Bob had hugged his daughter to his heart's content.

"As good as gold," said Bob, "and better. Somehow he gets thoughtful, sitting by himself so much, and thinks the strangest things you ever heard. He told me, coming home, that he hoped the people saw him in the church, because he was a cripple, and it might be pleasant to them to remember upon Christmas Day, who made lame beggars walk and blind men see."

Bob's voice was tremulous when he told them this, and trembled more when he said that Tiny Tim was growing strong and hearty.

His active little crutch was heard upon the floor, and back came Tiny Tim before another word was spoken, escorted by his brother and sister to his stool before the fire; and while Bob, turning up his cuffs— as if, poor fellow, they were capable of being made more shabby—compounded some hot mixture in a jug with gin and lemons, and stirred it round and round and put it on the hob to simmer, Master Peter and the two ubiquitous young Cratchits went to fetch the goose, with which they soon returned in high procession.

Such a bustle ensued that you might have thought a goose the rarest of all birds; a feathered phenomenon, to which a black swan was a matter of course, and in truth it was something very like it in that house. Mrs. Cratchit made the gravy (ready beforehand in a little saucepan) hissing hot; Master Peter mashed the potatoes with incredible vigor; Miss Belinda sweetened up the apple sauce; Martha dusted the hot plates; Bob took Tiny Tim beside him in a tiny corner at the table; the two young Cratchits set chairs for everybody, not forgetting themselves, and mounting guard upon their posts, crammed spoons into their mouths, lest they should shriek for goose before their turn came to be helped. At last the dishes were set on, and grace was said. It was succeeded by a breathless pause, as Mrs. Cratchit, looking slowly all along the carving-knife, prepared to plunge it in the beast; but when she did, and when the long-expected gush of stuffing issued forth, one murmur of delight arose all round the board, and even Tiny Tim, excited by the two young Cratchits, beat on the table with the handle of his knife, and feebly cried Hurrah!

There never was such a goose. Bob said he didn't believe there ever was such a goose cooked. Its tenderness and flavor, size and cheapness, were the themes of universal admiration. Eked out by the apple sauce and mashed potatoes, it was a sufficient dinner for the whole family; indeed, as Mrs. Cratchit said with great delight (surveying one small atom of a bone upon the dish), they hadn't ate it all at last! Yet everyone had had enough, and the youngest Cratchits, in particular, were seeped in sage and onion to the eyebrows! But now, the plates being changed by Miss Belinda, Mrs. Cratchit left the room alone—too nervous to bear witnesses—to take the pudding up and bring it in.

Suppose it should not be done enough! Suppose it should break in turning out! Suppose somebody should have got over the wall of the back-yard, and stolen it, while they were merry with the goose—a supposition at which the two young Cratchits became livid! All sorts of horrors were supposed.

Halloa! A great deal of steam! The pudding was out of the copper. A smell like a washing-day! That was the cloth. A smell like an eating-house and a pastry-cook's next door to each other, with a laundress's next door to that! That was the pudding! In half a minute Mrs. Cratchit entered—flushed, but smiling proudly—with the pudding, like a speckled cannonball, so hard and firm, blazing in half of half a quartern of ignited brandy, and bedight with Christmas holly stuck into the top.

Oh, a wonderful pudding! Bob Cratchit said, and calmly too, that he regarded it as the greatest success achieved by Mrs. Cratchit since their marriage. Mrs. Cratchit said that now the weight was off her mind, she would confess she had had her doubts about the quantity of flour. Everybody had something to say about it, but nobody said or thought it was at all a small pudding for a large family. It would have been flat heresy to do so. Any Cratchit would have blushed to hint at such a thing.

At last the dinner was all done, the cloth was cleared, the hearth swept, and the fire made up. The compound in the jug being tasted, and considered perfect, apples and oranges were put upon the table, and a shovelful of chestnuts on the fire. Then all the Cratchit family drew round the hearth in what Bob Cratchit called a circle, meaning half a one; and at Bob Cratchit's elbow stood the family display of glass. Two tumblers, and a custard-cup without a handle.

These held the hot stuff from the jug, however, as well as golden goblets would have done; and Bob served it out with beaming looks, while the chestnuts on the fire sputtered and cracked noisily. Then Bob proposed:

"A Merry Christmas to us all, my dears. God bless us!"

Which all the family re-echoed.

"God bless us every one!" said Tiny Tim, the last of all.

from *A Christmas Carol*

Christmas Day

*In those days a decree went out from Caesar Augustus that all the world should be enrolled. And all went to be enrolled, each to his own city. And Joseph also went up from Galilee, from the city of Nazareth, to Judea, to the city of David, which is called Bethlehem, to be enrolled with Mary, his betrothed.

And while they were there, the time came for her to be delivered. And she gave birth to her first-born son and wrapped him in swaddling cloths, and laid him in a manger, because there was no place for them in the inn.

And in that region there were shepherds out in the field, keeping watch over their flock by night. And an angel of the Lord appeared to them, and the glory of the Lord shone around them, and they were filled with fear.

And the angel said to them, "Be not afraid; for behold, I bring you good news of a great joy which will come to all the people; for to you is born this day in the city of David a Savior, who is Christ the Lord. And this will be a sign for you: you will find a babe wrapped in swaddling cloths and lying in a manger."

And suddenly there was with the angel a multitude of the heavenly host praising God and saying,

"Glory to God in the highest, and on earth peace among men with whom he is pleased!"

When the angels went away from them into heaven, the shepherds said to one another, "Let us go over to Bethlehem and see this thing that has happened, which the Lord has made known to us."

And they went with haste, and found Mary and Joseph, and the babe lying in a manger. And when they saw it they made known the saying which been told them concerning this child; and all who heard it wondered at what the shepherds told them. But Mary kept all these things, pondering them in her heart.

And the shepherds returned, glorifying and praising God for all they had heard and seen, as it had been told them.

[Luke 2:1, 3–20]

The
Carols

God Rest Ye Merry Gentlemen

Moderately

[Traditional English]

God rest ye mer - ry gen - tle - men, let noth - ing you dis -

mf

may. Re - mem - ber Christ our Sa - vior was born on Christ - mas

Day To save us all from Sa - tan's pow'r when we were gone a -

Refrain

stray O＿＿ tid - ings of com - fort and joy com - fort and

joy O＿＿ tid - ings of com - fort and joy. joy.

| 1-6 | 7 |

In Bethlehem, in Jewry,
This blessed Babe was born,
And laid within a manger,
Upon this blessed morn:
The which His Mother Mary
Did nothing take in score.
Refrain

From God our heavenly Father
A blessed angel came;
And unto certain Shepherds
Brought tidings of the same:
How that in Bethlehem was born
The Son of God by Name.
Refrain

"Fear not then," said the Angel,
"Let nothing you affright,
This day is born a Savior
Of a pure Virgin bright,
To free all those who trust in Him
From Satan's power and might.
Refrain

The shepherds at those tidings
Rejoiced much in mind,
And left their flocks a–feeding
In tempest, storm and wind:
And went to Bethlehem straightaway
The blessed Babe to find.
Refrain

And when they came to Bethlehem
Where our dear Savior lay,
They found Him in a manger,
Where oxen feed on hay:
His Mother Mary kneeling down,
Unto the Lord did pray.
Refrain

Now to the Lord sing praises,
All you within this place,
And with true love and brotherhood
Each other now embrace;
This holy tide of Christmas
All other doth deface.
Refrain

O Little Town of Bethlehem

PHILLIPS BROOKS

LEWIS H. REDNER

Moderately

O lit - tle town of Beth - le - hem, How still we — see thee lie! A -

bove thy deep and dream - less sleep The si - lent — stars go by. Yet

in thy dark streets shin - eth The ev - er - last - ing Light; The

hopes and fears of all the years Are met in thee to - night.

For Christ is born of Mary,	How silently, how silently	O holy Child of Bethlehem!
And gather'd all above,	The wondrous gift is giv'n!	Descend to us, we pray;
While mortals sleep, the angels keep	So God imparts to human hearts	Cast out our sin, and enter in,
Their watch of won-d'ring love.	The blessings of His heav'n.	Be born in us today.
O morning stars, together	No ear may hear His coming,	We hear the Christmas angels
Proclaim the holy birth!	But in this world of sin;	The great glad tidings tell;
And praises sing to God the King,	Where meek souls will receive Him still,	O come to us, abide with us,
And peace to men on earth!	The dear Christ enters in.	Our Lord Emmanuel!

Good King Wenceslas

JOHN MASON NEALE

Played with spirit

[Traditional]

Good King Wen - ces - las look'd out   On the Feast of Ste - phen,

When the snow lay round a - bout,   Deep, and crisp and e - ven.

Bright - ly shone the moon that night, Though the frost was cru - el,

When a poor man came in sight, Gath-'ring win - ter fu - el.

"Hither, page, and stand by me,
If thou know'st it, telling,
Yonder peasant, who is he?
Where and what his dwelling?"
"Sire, he lives a good league hence,
Underneath the mountain;
Right against the forest fence,
By Saint Agnes' fountain."

"Bring me flesh, and bring me wine,
Bring me pine-logs hither;
Thou and I will see him dine,
When we bear them thither."
Page and monarch forth they went,
Forth they went together;
Through the rude winds wild lament:
And the bitter weather.

"Sire, the night is darker now,
And the wind blows stronger;
Fails my heart, I know not how,
I can go not longer."
"Mark my footsteps, my good page,
Tread thou in them boldly:
Thou shalt find the winter's rage
Freeze thy blood less coldly."

In his master's steps he trod,
Where the snow lay dinted;
Heat was in the very sod
Which the saint had printed.
Therefore, Christian men, be sure,
Wealth or rank possessing,
Ye who now will bless the poor,
Shall yourselves find blessing.

Hark! The Herald Angels Sing

CHARLES WESLEY FELIX MENDELSSOHN

Stately

Hark! the her - ald an - gels sing __ Glo - ry to the new - born King;

Peace on earth, and mer - cy mild, __ God and sin - ners re - con - ciled!

Joy - ful all ye na - tions rise, __ Join the tri - umph of the skies; __

With th'an-gel - ic host pro - claim, Christ is __ born in Beth - le - hem.

Refrain

Hark! the her - ald an - gels sing, Glo - ry __ to the new - born King.

ff

Christ, by highest heav'n adored;
Christ, the everlasting Lord;
Late in time behold Him come,
Off-spring of the Virgin's womb.
Veil'd in flesh the God-head see;
Hail th'Incarnate Deity,
Pleased as Man with man to dwell,
Jesus, our Emmanuel!
Refrain

Mild He lays His glory by,
Born that man no more may die,
Born to raise the sons of earth,
Born to give them second birth.
Ris'n with healing in His wings,
Light and life to all He brings,
Hail, the sun of Righteousness!
Hail the heav'n born Prince of Peace!
Refrain

Joy to the World

ISAAC WATTS

GEORGE FREDERICK HANDEL WITH LOWELL MASON

Majestically

Joy to the world! the Lord is come; Let

earth re - ceive her King; _____ Let

ev - 'ry ___ heart ___ pre - pare ___ Him ___ room ___ And

heav'n and na - ture _ sing, And _ heav'n and na - ture _ sing, And _

heav'n ___ and heav'n ___ and na - ture sing.

Joy to the world! the Savior reigns;
Let men their songs employ;
While fields and floods, rocks, hills, and plains
Repeat the sounding joy,
Repeat the sounding joy,
Repeat, repeat the sounding joy.

He rules the world with truth and grace
And makes the nations prove
The glories of His righteousness
And wonders of His love,
And wonders of His love,
And wonders, and wonders of His love.

The Twelve Days of Christmas

THE FIRST DAY OF CHRISTMAS

[Traditional English]

On the first day of Christ - mas my true love sent to me A

par - tridge ___ in a pear tree.

THE SECOND DAY OF CHRISTMAS

On the sec - ond day of Christ - mas my true love sent to me

Two tur - tle doves And a par - tridge — in a pear tree.

THE THIRD DAY OF CHRISTMAS

On the third day of Christ - mas my true love sent to me

Three French — hens, Two tur - tle doves And a par - tridge — in a pear tree.

THE FOURTH DAY OF CHRISTMAS

On the fourth day of Christ - mas my true love sent to me

Four call - ing birds, Three French _ hens, Two tur - tle doves And a

par - tridge _____ in a pear tree.

THE FIFTH-TWELFTH DAYS OF CHRISTMAS

On the fifth day of Christ - mas my true love sent to me [to ⑤]
On the sixth day of Christ - mas my true love sent to me [to ⑥]
On the sev - enth day of Christ - mas my true love sent to me [to ⑦]
On the eighth day of Christ - mas my true love sent to me [to ⑧]
On the ninth day of Christ - mas my true love sent to me [to ⑨]
On the tenth day of Christ - mas my true love sent to me [to ⑩]
On the 'lev - enth day of Christ - mas my true love sent to me [to ⑪]
On the twelfth day of Christ - mas my true love sent to me [to ⑫]

Twelve drum - mers drum - ming, 'lev - en pi - pers pi - ping, Ten lords a - leap - ing,

Nine la - dies danc - ing, Eight maids a - milk - ing, Sev - en swans a - swim - ming,

O Christmas Tree
(O TANNENBAUM)

[Traditional German]

Moderately

O Christ-mas tree, O Christ-mas tree! Your boughs are so un - chang - ing;

Thy branch - es green in sum - mer time, And through the snows of

win - ter's clime; O Christ-mas tree, O Christ-mas tree! Your boughs are so un - chang - ing.

O Christmas Tree! O Christmas Tree!
Much pleasure thou can'st give me;
How often has the Christmas tree
Afforded me the greatest glee!
O Christmas Tree! O Christmas Tree!
Much pleasure thou can'st give me.

O Christmas Tree! O Christmas Tree!
Thy candles shine so brightly!
From base to summit gay and bright,
There's only splendor for the sight.
O Christmas Tree! O Christmas Tree!
Thy candles shine so brightly!

O Christmas Tree! O Christmas Tree!
How richly God has decked thee!
Thou bidst us true and faithful be,
And trust in God unchangingly.
O Christmas Tree! O Christmas Tree!
How richly God has decked thee!

59

It Came upon a Midnight Clear

EDMUND HAMILTON SEARS

RICHARD STORRS WILLIS

Moderately

It came up-on a mid-night clear, That glo-rious song of old, From

an - gels bend - ing near the earth To touch their harps _ of gold: _____ "Peace

on the earth, _ good - will to men From heav'n's _ all gra - cious King." ___ The

world in sol - emn still - ness lay To hear the an - gels sing. _____

Still through the cloven skies they come,
With peaceful wings unfurl'd,
And still their heav'nly music floats
O'er all the weary world:
Above its sad and lowly plains
They bend on hov'ring wing,
And ever o'er its Babel sounds
The blessed angels sing.

O ye, beneath life's crushing load,
Whose forms are bending low,
Who toil along the climbing way
With painful steps and slow!
Look now, for glad and golden hours
Come swiftly on the wing;
O rest beside the weary road,
And hear the angels sing.

For lo! the days are hast'ning on,
By prophets seen of old,
When with the ever circling years
Shall come the time foretold,
When the new heav'n and earth shall own
The Prince of Peace, their King,
And the whole world send back the song
Which now the angels sing.

We Wish You a Merry Christmas

tid - ings for Christ - mas And a Hap - py New Year!

Please bring us some figgy pudding,	We won't go until we get some,	We wish you a Merry Christmas,
Please bring us some figgy pudding,	We won't go until we get some,	We wish you a Merry Christmas,
Please bring us some figgy pudding,	We won't go until we get some,	We wish you a Merry Christmas
Please bring it right here!	Please bring it right here!	And a Happy New Year!
Refrain	*Refrain*	*Refrain*

The Wassail Song

Lively

[Traditional English]

Here we come a - was - sail - ing A - mong the leaves so green, _____

Here we come a wan - d'ring, So fair _____ to be seen. Love and

Refrain

joy come to you, And to you your was-sail too, And God bless you And send___ you a hap-py new year, And God send you a hap-py new___ year.

We are not daily beggars
That beg from door to door,
But we are neighbors' children
Whom you have seen before.
Refrain

Good master and good mistress,
As you sit by the fire,
Pray think of us poor children
Who wander in the mire.
Refrain

We have a little purse
Made of ratching leather skin;
We want some of your small change
To line it well within.
Refrain

Bring us out a table
And spread it with a cloth;
Bring us out a cheese,
And of your Christmas loaf.
Refrain

God bless the master of this house,
Likewise the mistress too;
And all the little children
That round the table go.
Refrain

Away in a Manger

JAMES R. MURRAY

A - way in a man - ger, no crib for His bed, The

lit - tle Lord Je - sus laid down His sweet head; The

stars in the heav - ens looked down where He lay, The

lit - tle Lord   Je - sus   a - sleep   in   the   hay.

The cattle are lowing the poor baby wakes,
But little Lord Jesus no crying He makes;
I love Thee, Lord Jesus, look down from the sky,
And stay by my cradle 'till morning is nigh.

Be near me, Lord Jesus, I ask Thee to stay
Close by me forever and love me, I pray;
Bless all the dear children in thy tender care,
And take us to heaven to live with Thee there.

The First Nowell

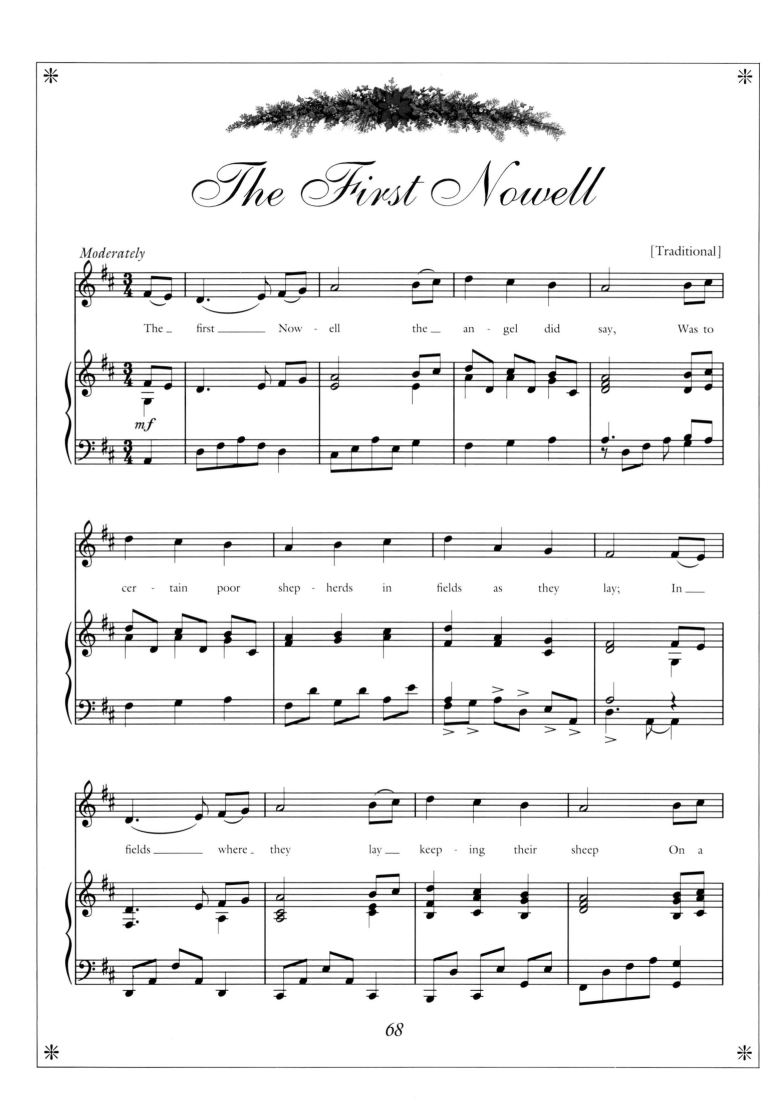

Moderately

[Traditional]

The _ first _____ Now - ell the _ an - gel did say, Was to

cer - tain poor shep - herds in fields as they lay; In _____

fields _____ where _ they lay _ keep - ing their sheep On a

Refrain

cold win-ter's night ____ that was ____ so deep. Now -

ell, _____ Now - ell, Now - ell, Now - ell,

Born is the King ____ of Is - ra - el.

They looked up and saw a star
Shining in the East beyond them far,
And to the earth it gave great light,
And so it continued both day and night.
Refrain

This star drew nigh to the North West,
O'er Bethlehem it took its rest,
And there it did both stop and stay
Right over the place where Jesus lay.
Refrain

Then enter'd in there Wise men three,
Full rev'rently on bended knee,
And offer'd there in His presence,
Their gold and myrrh and frankincense.
Refrain

Deck the Hall

[Traditional Welsh]

Deck the hall with boughs of hol - ly, Fa la la la la la la la la.

'Tis the sea - son to be jol - ly, Fa la la la la la la la la.

Don we now our gay ap - par - el, Fa la la la la la la la la.

Troll the an-cient Yule-tide car-ol, Fa la la la la la la la la.

Fa la la la la la la la la.

ff

See the blazing Yule before us,
Fa la la la la la la la la.
Strike the harp and join the chorus,
Fa la la la la la la la la.
Follow me in merry measure,
Fa la la la la la la la la.
While I tell of Yuletide treasure,
Fa la la la la la la la la.

Fast away the old year passes,
Fa la la la la la la la la.
Hail the new, ye lads and lasses,
Fa la la la la la la la la.
Sing we joyous all together,
Fa la la la la la la la la.
Heedless of the wind and weather,
Fa la la la la la la la la.

Silent Night

JOSEPH MOHR   FRANZ GRUBER

Slowly with feeling

Si - lent night! Ho - ly night!

All is calm, all is bright:

'Round yon Vir - gin Moth - er and Child,

Holy Infant, so tender and mild,

Sleep in heav - en - ly peace,

Sleep in heav - en - ly peace.

Silent night! Holy night!
Shepherds quake at the sight!
Glories stream from heaven afar,
Heav'nly hosts sing Alleluia;
Christ, the Savior, is born,
Christ, the Savior, is born.

Silent night! Holy night!
Son of God, love's pure light
Radiant beams from Thy holy face
With the dawn of redeeming grace,
Jesus, Lord, at Thy birth,
Jesus, Lord, at Thy birth.

O Holy Night

JOHN SULLIVAN DWIGHT   ADOLPHE CHARLES ADAM

Slowly with feeling

O ho - ly night! __ the stars are bright - ly

shin - ing, It is the night of the dear Sav - ior's birth;

Long lay the world _____ in sin and er - ror

pin - ing, Till He ap - peared and the soul felt its

worth. A thrill of hope the

wea - ry world re - joic - es, For yon - der breaks _____ a

new and glo - rious morn. _____ Fall on your

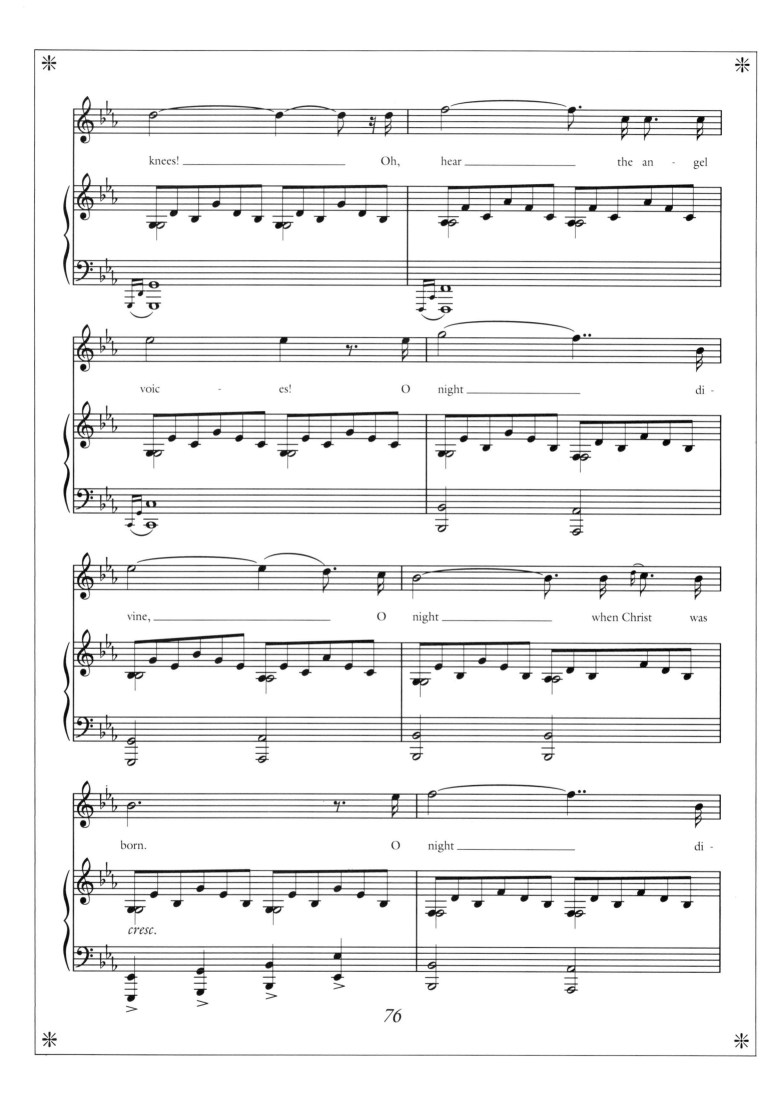

knees! _____ Oh, hear _____ the an - gel

voic - es! O night _____ di -

vine, _____ O night _____ when Christ was

born. O night _____ di -

cresc.

76

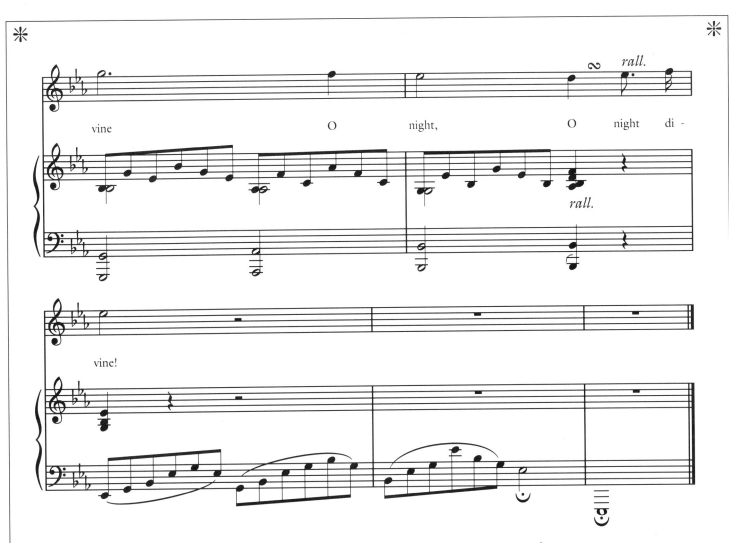

vine   O   night,   O   night di-

rall.

rall.

vine!

Led by the light of stars serenely beaming,
With glowing hearts by His cradle we stand;
So led by light of a star sweetly gleaming
Here came the wise men from Orient land.
The King of kings lay thus in lowly manger,
In all our trials born to be our friend.

He knows our need,
Our weakness is no stranger
Behold your King!
Before Him lowly bend.
Behold your King!
Before Him bend!

O Come, All Ye Faithful
(ADESTE FIDELES)

JOHN FRANCIS WADE (Latin)
FREDERICK OAKELEY (English)

JOHN READING

Sing, choirs of angels,
Sing with exultations,
Sing, all ye citizens of heav'n above:
Glory to God in the highest;
Refrain

Yea, Lord, we greet Thee,
Born this happy morning,
Jesus, to Thee be glory giv'n;
Word of the Father,
Now in flesh appearing;
Refrain

What Child Is This?

WILLIAM CHATTERTON DIX

What Child is this, _____ Who, laid to rest, _____ On Ma - ry's lap _____ is

sleep - ing? Whom an - gels greet _____ with an - thems sweet, _____ While

shep - herds watch ___ are keep - ing? This, this ___ is

Christ the King; ___ Whom shep - herds guard ___ and an - gels sing:

Haste, haste ___ to bring Him laud, ___ The Babe, ___ the Son ___ of Ma - ry!

Why lies He in such mean estate,
Where ox and ass are feeding?
Good Christian, fear: for sinners here
The silent Word is pleading.
Nails, spear, shall pierce Him through,
The Cross be borne, for me, for you:
Hail, hail the Word made flesh,
The Babe, the Son of Mary!

So bring Him incense, gold and myrrh,
Come peasant, king, to own Him;
The King of kings, salvation brings;
Let loving hearts enthrone Him.
Raise, raise the song on high,
The Virgin sings her lullaby:
Joy, joy for Christ is born,
The Babe, the Son of Mary!

Jingle Bells

JAMES PIERPONT

fun it is to ride and sing A sleigh-ing song to-night!

Refrain

Jin - gle Bells! Jin - gle Bells! Jin - gle all the way!

Oh, what fun it is to ride In a one horse o - pen sleigh! one horse o - pen sleigh!

Day or two ago
I thought I'd take a ride,
And soon Miss Fannie Bright
Was seated by my side.
The horse was lean and lank,
Misfortune seemed his lot,
He got into a drifted bank,
And we, we got up sot.
Refrain

Now the ground is white,
Go it while you're young;
Take the girls tonight
And sing this sleighing song;
Just get a bobtail nag,
Two forty for his speed,
Then hitch him to an open sleigh,
And crack! you'll take the lead.
Refrain

Go Tell It on the Mountain

Freely

[Negro Spiritual]

While shep-herds kept their watch-ing O'er si-lent flocks by night, Be-

Not too fast
Refrain

hold through-out the hea-vens, There shone a ho-ly light: Oh!

Go tell it on the moun - tain, O - ver the hills and ev - 'ry-where;

Go tell it on the moun - tain That Je - sus Christ is born!

Je - sus Christ is born!

The shepherds feared and trembled
When lo! above the earth
Rang out the angel chorus
That hailed Our Savior's birth:
Refrain

Down in a lowly manger
Our humble Christ was born
And God sent us salvation,
That blessed Christmas morn:
Refrain

When I was a seeker,
I sought both night and day;
I sought the Lord to help me,
And He showed me the way:
Refrain

He made me a watchman
Upon the city wall,
And if I am a Christian,
I am the least of all.
Refrain

Angels We Have Heard on High

Joyously

[Traditional]

An - gels we have heard on high, Sweet - ly sing - ing o'er the plains.

And the moun - tains in re - ply, Ech - o - ing their joy - ous strains.

Refrain

Glo — — — — — — — — ri - a

Shepherds, why this jubilee?
Why your joyous strains prolong?
What the gladsome tidings be,
Which inspire your heav'nly song?
Refrain

Come, to Bethlehem, and see
Him whose birth the angels sing;
Come, adore on bended knee,
Christ the Lord, the newborn King.
Refrain

See Him in a manger laid,
Whom the choirs of angels praise;
Mary, Joseph lend your aid,
While our hearts in love we raise.
Refrain

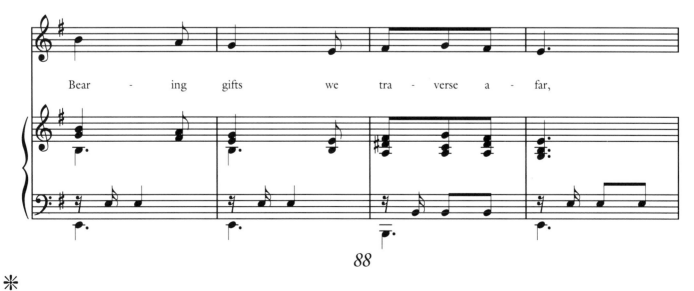

We Three Kings of Orient Are

JOHN HENRY HOPKINS

Moderately

We three kings of O - ri - ent are;

mf

Bear - ing gifts we tra - verse a - far,

Field and foun - tain, moor and moun - tain,

Fol - low - ing yon - der star.

Refrain

O _____

star of won - der star of night,

Star with roy - al beau - ty bright,

West - ward lead - ing, still pro - ceed - ing,

Guide us to Thy per - fect light.

Born a King on Bethlehem's plain,
Gold we bring, to crown Him again,
King forever, ceasing never,
Over us all to reign.
Refrain

Frankincense to offer have I,
Incense owns a Deity nigh.
Pray'r and praising, all men raising,
Worship Him, God most High.
Refrain

Myrrh is mine, its bitter perfume,
Breathes a life of gathering gloom;
Sorrowing, sighing, bleeding, dying,
Sealed in the stone cold tomb.
Refrain

Glorious now behold Him arise,
King and God and Sacrifice,
Hallelujah, Hallelujah,
Earth to heav'n replies.
Refrain